YOUR PRACTICAL GUIDE

for Saving, Spending
and Investing

Help, Hope and Insight for Your
Money *and* Your Life

CROWN

Chuck Bentley and Larry Burkett

ISBN 978-1-56427-313-0

Verses identified as (NIV) are taken from the *Holy Bible: New International Version*, ©1973, 1978, 1984 by the International Bible Society. Used by permission of Zondervan Bible Publishers.

Verses identified as (TLB) are taken from *The Living Bible*, ©1971 by Tyndale House Publishers, Wheaton, Illinois. Used by permission.

All other Scripture quotations are taken from the *New American Standard Bible*® (Updated Edition) (NASB), ©1960, 1962, 1963, 1968, 1971, 1972, 1973, 1975, 1977, 1995 by The Lockman Foundation. Used by permission.

MoneyLife™ is a trademark of Crown Financial Ministries.

CONTENTS

INTRODUCTION

Help and Hope Are Here.

Whether you are in prevention mode—prudently planning to avoid financial pressure—or in repair mode—scrambling to escape its clutches, **Crown exists to provide help, hope, and insight.** These Help and Hope buttons appear whenever special information is available to assist and encourage you.

This book, rather than a comprehensive study, is a brief but powerful analysis that will enable you to apply God's wisdom to your situation. It will also give you resources for further study in any of the topics you choose.

Regardless of your present circumstances, you can experience abundant life as you practice financial faithfulness. God may choose to bless you with wealth or He may not, but He clearly wants you to have abundant life, joy, peace, and freedom from fear and worry. No amount of money can buy these benefits.

As you learn and apply God's principles, you will see His hand at work in your circumstances. We've included stories of real people who have taken the same kind of journey you're beginning. Let their experience encourage you to submit to God's direction so you can feel His wind at your back. Let the journey begin!

Please notice a few helpful features:

1. Appendix 1 is an introduction to Christ. If you (or someone you know) are uncertain about where you stand with God, this short introduction will guide you into an intimate relationship with Him.

2. Appendix 2, "God's Ownership & Financial Faithfulness," briefly explores a fundamental concept—one that frames the correct perspective on every financial principle in Scripture. If you don't understand this, you are likely to manage your resources with worldly wisdom. The world's approach to money management isn't always evil, but it is short-sighted (ignoring eternity), incomplete (ignoring the Creator/Controller/Provider), and usually in pursuit of the wrong goals.

3. Because we are committed to transformation rather than mere information, each chapter ends with a two-part exercise:

   • An Action Step you create based on your response to the chapter

   • A Celebration Plan for every Action Step completed

Please take advantage of these to maximize your experience in this book. James 1:22 sums it up when it says, *"Do not merely listen to the word, and so deceive yourselves. Do what it says"* (NIV).

HELP, HOPE, AND INSIGHT SERIES | BOOK 1

SECTION ONE

DEBT AND BANKRUPTCY

Bad news: The consequences of debt, bankruptcy and gambling threaten all of us, either directly or indirectly.

Good news: God's desire for us is to experience the abundant life:
"I [Jesus] came that they may have life, and have it abundantly" (John 10:10).

We can follow God's direction or we can try to shortcut it. Gambling and the abuse of consumer credit are shortcuts that advertise the abundant life but lead to a distorted version of it: one that often ends in bankruptcy. Or chronic discontent. Or missing the best God has for us. Or all three.

God has given us ample direction for experiencing this abundant life, and we want to share this good news with you.

CHAPTER 1

DEBT & CREDIT

In the world of your money life, the big picture could be called "financial faithfulness."

Credit is potential, and potential is good. Until it goes bad.

If you've ever had to repair your credit, you've probably become more sensitive to its importance and what you need to do to protect it. We want to help you keep it good because your reputation depends on it. *"A good name is more desirable than great riches; to be esteemed is better than silver or gold"* (Proverbs 22:1, NIV).

Our consumer-driven economy sustains itself by creating attractive products and convincing us they are needs. Its use of advertising has evolved into something much more than product education and business promotion; it feeds the illusion that we can capture the good life through the accumulation of more stuff.

Fifty years ago no one could have imagined today's easy-credit culture with its buy-now-pay-later allure. Compulsive impatience has become the hallmark of the shopper with money to burn—even if the money hasn't actually arrived yet.

Although credit is not evil, its attraction invites abuse, and that leads to getting hooked. Since taking the bait usually results from misunderstanding the nature of the lure, let's take a moment to define a few crucial terms.

1. **Credit:** "the establishment of a mutual trust relationship between a lender and a borrower (or potential borrower)." So far, so good. A trust relationship is a wonderful thing.

2. **Debt:** "something owed." Now the potential (credit) has become an obligation (debt) we must repay. This applies to every instance of routine borrowing. Scripture never prohibits debt, but it does require us to repay anything we owe. Since we have defined debt as simply "something owed," let's make one clarification. Regular payments for services such as utilities are "something owed," but we do not consider them debt unless they become past due.

3. **Adequate collateral:** "something of value pledged as a guarantee of repayment." This could be any kind of asset (land, house, car, etc.) with enough value to satisfy the lender's claim against you if you are unable to repay as agreed. Although you may not be required to physically deliver the asset to the lender until the loan is paid in full, think of the asset as being under house arrest—you can't take it out and pledge it somewhere else.

4. **Surety debt:** "a loan without adequate collateral to satisfy the agreement if payments cannot be maintained." This is the kind of debt the Bible warns us to avoid. If unexpected circumstances cause us to default, we can lose everything. *"Do not be among those who give pledges, among those who become guarantors [sureties] for debts. If you have nothing with which to pay, why should he take your bed from under you?"* (Proverbs 22:26-27).

Surety debt has become a way of life in recent decades. The alarming rise in bankruptcies shows how the lure of easy credit has hooked people. They never anticipated being unable to fulfill their agreement to repay. Consider these examples of surety debt.

- A mortgage with a low (or no) down payment seems like a clever way to leverage other people's money—until adjustable rates rise or a job is lost or some other emergency prohibits timely payments.

- Buying a car without at least 20 percent down. If we miss payments, repossession of the car does not satisfy the lender's right to what we promised. We will be obligated to find a bundle of cash to make up the difference between the greatly depreciated value of the car and the high loan balance.

- Furniture and other consumer loans that require little or no down payment.

- Unsecured loans of all kinds unless we have cash saved to repay them if necessary. Education loans fit into this category, although they are reasonably justified on the basis of enhanced earning power. It is still prudent to keep them at the lowest possible level.

Many families—even young couples—have built surety debts into a pyramid totaling hundreds of thousands of dollars. A pyramid may stand on its head for a while, but sooner or later a tremor, a gust of wind or even a big ant sneeze will bring it crashing down.

If a mortgage can be surety debt, does this mean we should never have a mortgage? The simple answer is to make sure the house (or asset serving as collateral) has a liquidation value higher than the loan against it. We'll explain further in a minute.

We would like to think Christians avoid surety debt because we take our direction from God's Word rather than from the world. But we can't always use the church's example as our cue, since the average American church is as deeply in debt as the average American business—and with about the same rate of delinquent payments and bankruptcies.

The most reliable source of wisdom is the Word of God. Its timeless truth guides us to the balance we need today as surely as it guided Israel through the wilderness. Their problems, like ours, grew out of their willingness to ignore it.

God's Word suggests that His plan for us is to be debt-free and, even better, that we should have the wealth to be lenders rather than borrowers. *"The Lord will open for you His good storehouse, the heavens, to give rain to your land in its season and to bless all the work of your hand; and you shall lend to many nations, but you shall not borrow"* (Deuteronomy 28:12).

The burdens of debt go far beyond our finances, extending to every part of our life. We find it difficult to focus our Bible study, meditation and prayer on becoming more Christlike when the pyramid over our heads is teetering. And the effects of financial bondage on a marriage relationship are measurable in the statistics of failed marriages. About 80 percent of divorced couples list finances as the leading cause of their downfall.

Thankfully, we can also say that the blessings of debt-free living will benefit every part of life, reducing stress and increasing our ability to enjoy God's provision.

While we strive to prevent people from going into surety debt, we realize that many are already under the shadow of the pyramid. God's Word offers guidance to them as well. We want to affirm that anyone—with desire, discipline, and time—can become debt free and stay that way. If becoming debt free is your desire, God will help you make it happen regardless of your current financial situation. Do your part, and trust Him to do His part!

What Does the Bible Say about Borrowing?

The Bible gives some very practical principles concerning borrowing. Remember that these are principles, not laws.

- **Principles** are instructions from the Lord to help guide our decisions.

- **Laws** are more than instructions; they are absolute directives.

Ignoring a **principle** may result in negative consequences, but ignoring a God-given **law** will likely result in punishment.

A biblical **principle** of borrowing is that it is better not to take on surety debt, personally assuring repayment without a guaranteed means (adequate collateral) of paying it. *"A man lacking in sense pledges and becomes guarantor [surety] in the presence of his neighbor"* (Proverbs 17:18).

A biblical **law** of borrowing is that it is a sin to borrow and not repay. *"The wicked borrows and does not pay back, but the righteous is gracious and gives"* (Psalm 37:21). The assumption in the verse is that the wicked person can repay but will not, as opposed to an individual who wants to repay but cannot.

God gives principles to keep us clearly within His path so we can experience His full blessings. Ignoring them puts us in a constant state of jeopardy as we wander, like the Israelites, stumbling over every temptation Satan puts in our way.

Some have taught that Romans 13:8 is a law against all forms of borrowing: *"Owe nothing to anyone except to love one another; for he who loves his neighbor has fulfilled the law."*

The context, however, is a transition from Paul's summation of our duty to submit to authority and pay everyone what we owe them (including taxes). He then urges us to obey the great love command by calling it a lifelong debt, one we can never fully repay.

Neither this verse nor any other is a *law* against borrowing. The Bible does not prohibit debt, but it offers principles that discourage and limit it.

How does a Person Establish Credit?

Imagine taking a young girl off a bicycle, setting her on a Harley and saying, "You go, girl!" Our easy-credit culture allows young people to qualify for much more credit than they can handle. Disaster waits around the corner.

> THE MOST RELIABLE SOURCE OF WISDOM IS THE WORD OF GOD.

The best way to establish credit is to borrow against an acceptable asset (adequate collateral). For example, if we have saved $1,000 and want to borrow the same amount, almost any bank will lend us $1,000 using the savings as collateral. Since the lender will probably charge two percent more than the prevailing savings rate, it will cost about $20 for a one-year loan to establish a good credit history.

It is also possible to get a secured credit card—one that is tied to a savings account and limited to the amount in the account.

Then, by using the bank as a credit reference, almost anyone can qualify for a major credit card with at least a small credit limit. This is not a suggestion to rush out and apply for a credit card or an assurance that the person can manage one properly. The point is that credit is relatively simple to establish if we have already acquired the discipline of saving.

Having a relative or friend cosign for a loan is a common way to establish credit, but it is also a form of surety to be avoided. *"Do not be among those who give pledges, among those who become guarantors [sureties] for debts"* (Proverbs 22:26).

How Can We Borrow and Avoid Surety Debt?

Remember our definition of surety debt: "a loan without adequate collateral to satisfy the agreement if payments cannot be maintained." It is taking on an obligation without an absolutely certain way to repay.

Suppose we want to buy a car costing $10,000. We put $2,000 down and sign a note for $8,000, pledging the car as collateral and guaranteeing the note by signing a deficiency agreement. Of course, we wouldn't realize we have signed a deficiency agreement unless we read the fine print, but it's there! We have just created a surety debt because if we are unable to make the payments, the car is repossessed and sold (usually at a loss), and we are required to make up the difference (the deficiency).

If we refuse to sign the deficiency agreement we would not be creating a surety debt. But we probably wouldn't get the car either, because the lender isn't likely to make the loan without it.

If, however, we had a substantially larger down payment (meaning a smaller loan), we could assure ourselves that the car's liquidation value would fully cover any remaining balance.

Common conditions and attitudes that lead to debt:

1. **Ignorance**—Many of us never had any training, either formal or by example, to manage money.

2. **Indulgence**—Modern culture feeds the impulse to spend, spend, spend. If you don't have it, get it. If you can't afford it, get it anyway; you deserve it.

3. **Impatience**—We tend to think we have a "right" to at least two new cars, a nice home and exciting vacations—NOW! The con-

cept of starting out small and patiently building our lifestyle one step at a time seems quaint by modern standards.

4. **Poor planning**—No matter how noble our intentions, if we have no spending plan that prioritizes expenses and balances them with our income, we are on the road to financial nightmares.

How to Get out of Debt

Proverbs 22:3 says, *"The prudent sees the evil and hides himself, but the naive go on, and are punished for it"* (NIV). Remember, anyone—with desire, discipline, and time—can become debt free and stay that way. Follow these steps to get out of debt.

1. **Stop any form of borrowing.** This includes credit cards! Consumer credit is our most common source of indebtedness, and the sooner you stop borrowing, the sooner you will get out of debt.

2. **Develop a spending plan.** A spending plan is not a straitjacket; it is a thoughtful strategy that simplifies daily decisions and ensures that your priorities will be met. The deeper in debt you are, the more restrictive your spending plan will need to be for at least a year—maybe longer. Crown offers many valuable resources to help you create a successful spending plan. Go to Crown.org for more information.

3. **Work out a payback plan with your creditors.** Most creditors are willing to work with people who honestly want to repay them. Visit Crown.org for some online tools to help you create a payback plan.

4. **Learn to trust God** for the things you truly need but can't afford. God may not want you to have an item you thought was a need but was really only a desire.

5. **Exercise self-discipline as a lifestyle.** Curb your impulses to buy. If it's not in your spending plan, don't buy it.

6. **Seek counsel.** Many of us need assistance with establishing and maintaining a spending plan and working with creditors.

In summary, strive to base your decisions on the principles of God's Word rather than the world's conventional "wisdom." God wants us to live debt free in order to serve Him to our utmost. If you are in debt, determine now to get out and stay out. With God's help you can do it!

QUESTIONS AND ANSWERS

This next section contains answers to debt and credit questions raised by our listeners and readers.

We owe money to several creditors and are having trouble deciding which to pay first—we just can't pay them all. Do you think a bill consolidation loan would help our situation?

The thought of paying off multiple high-interest-rate creditors with one lower-rate loan is very appealing. The problem is that a consolidation loan may treat the symptoms for a while, but unless a disciplined and diligent lifestyle is adopted, greater bondage soon follows.

> CREDIT IS RELATIVELY SIMPLE TO ESTABLISH IF WE HAVE ALREADY ACQUIRED THE DISCIPLINE OF SAVING.

The vast majority of people who take a consolidation loan—usually by tapping into home equity—pay off their credit cards only to accumulate the same amount of credit card debt within two years. But this time, they are also making the large consolidation loan payments. And they have burned their equity! A well isn't worth much when it's dry.

Consolidation loans should never be the first step in resolving a debt problem. First create a spending plan and develop the discipline to stick with it.

Continue making the minimum payments on all your debts, but focus on accelerating the payment of your smallest higher-interest debt first.

Then, after you pay off the first one, apply its payment toward the next smallest one. After the second one is paid off, apply what you were paying on the first and second toward the third smallest one, and so forth. The encouragement of seeing debts retired and a growing amount that you can add to your remaining payments gives you great momentum. Visit us online at Crown.org and use the available online calculators that can help create a payback plan.

A lower-interest consolidation loan might work for you but only after you've established a spending plan and the discipline to maintain it.

According to the Bible, shouldn't I be released from my debts after six years?

Don't we wish! In Deuteronomy 15:1-2, there is an admonition not to lend money for a period of more than six years, but this does not apply to borrowers. If you borrow, you must repay regardless of how long the debt extends.

I fully pay my credit card bills each month and have no debts other than my home mortgage, but my brother says that Christians should not use credit cards at all. Is he right?

Proverbs 22:3 says, *"The prudent sees the evil and hides himself, but the naive go on, and are punished for it"* (NIV). Credit and credit cards are not the problem; misuse of credit is the problem. Use these simple rules for credit cards.

1. Never use your credit cards for anything that isn't in your spending plan.

2. Pay your credit cards off every month.

3. The first month you cannot pay off your credit card in full, cut it up. You've just proved it's too dangerous for you.

4. Finally, keep in mind that being able to afford something doesn't necessarily mean you should buy it.

Our son is going off to college next fall. Since the school is several hundred miles away, would it be a good idea to give him a credit card to use to travel home and for emergencies?

The idea has merit—as long as your son is well trained and disciplined, and you keep a careful eye on the statements. Otherwise, it's like pouring gas on glowing embers. Unfortunately, "well trained and disciplined" is the exception rather than the rule in spite of our oft-quoted *"Train up a child in the way he should go, even when he is old he will not depart from it"* (Proverbs 22:6).

The two greatest risks are:

1. He may give in to the temptation to indulge himself (and his friends) at your expense.

2. Even worse, the false security provided by "easy money" through credit often translates into undisciplined spending habits later in life.

Only you can evaluate your son's level of training, experience and discipline. As you pray about this decision, ask for God's wisdom. *"If any of you lacks wisdom, let him ask of God, who gives to all generously and without reproach, and it will be given to him"* (James 1:5).

I am working with a financial counselor to set up a plan to pay

off my creditors, but I am still being hounded by collection agencies. Is there any way to get these guys off my case?

The Consumer Protection Act of 1986 gives a measure of relief from harassment by unscrupulous collection agents. Calls late at night or very early in the morning are prohibited, as well as calls to your place of employment if you have notified the agency that your employer disapproves. A collection agent may not misrepresent himself or provide false information or threaten legal action when none is intended. If you believe an agent or agency is in violation of this Act, contact the Federal Trade Commission in Washington, D.C., for further information on any recourse you may have.

My wife and I are so far in debt that we see no way out other than bankruptcy. Does the Bible prohibit us from filing?

This is not a simple question to answer. God's Word is clear about us being responsible for our promises and repaying what we owe. *"When you make a vow to God, do not be late in paying it; for He takes no delight in fools. Pay what you vow! It is better that you should not vow than that you should vow and not pay"* (Ecclesiastes 5:4-5).

Does this mean that in the interim people should not take the legal remedy of court protection that would allow them to get reestablished so they can regain the ability to pay what they promised? That is an individual decision, but we must never lose sight of the paramount requirement to repay everyone what we owe. Satisfying a legal requirement doesn't relieve our responsibility to fulfill a moral obligation. Just remember that God is more than willing to help you as you trust Him and apply His principles in your finances.

My husband is owner of a small business. Due to the economy in our area, we have suffered terrific losses and the business owes a lot of money. We have been counseled to file for bankruptcy. Is that right?

Psalms 37:21 says, *"The wicked borrows and does not pay back, but the righteous is gracious and gives."* God's Word doesn't distinguish between a personal debt and a business debt. When you borrow money for any purpose, you make a vow (or promise) to repay what you borrowed. In the short run, you may have to live a very frugal life, and it may not seem fair; but in the long run you will have obeyed God. Nothing else will matter 100 years from now.

This is not to say that you shouldn't seek court protection until you are able to set up a repayment plan. That is an individual decision between you and God.

Does the Bible prohibit a Christian from borrowing money from a non-Christian?

God's Word simply says that whatever is borrowed must be repaid. It doesn't specify whether a believer should borrow from another believer or from a nonbeliever. It doesn't make any difference, as far as repayment is concerned. A caution appears in Proverbs 22:7 in which we are told that a lender becomes an authority over a borrower. That could be a problem for a church or ministry if a lender tried to exercise influence over policies or operations.

A Jaguar, a Radio, and Gardening Shoes
The story of Kevin Cross

"It's amazing how God uses any medium to get your attention, even listening to the radio in someone else's car for just a couple of minutes," says Kevin Cross. "But all He needs is one moment to really change a person's heart."

Kevin's change of heart occurred when he reached the bottom—spiritually, emotionally, and financially—as a young man trying to survive in south Florida in the late 1980s.

Just a few years before, at age 19, he'd been awarded a scholarship to law school that covered half of his expenses. But instead of making him thankful, the scholarship fed his thinking that he was the "boy wonder."

He began using credit cards recklessly, adding to the student loan debt he'd incurred to pay the other half of his college expenses. He also violated school policies by taking money to do homework assignments for other students.

His debt continued climbing until it reached $100,000. After one year in law school, he was asked to take a leave of absence—because of legal troubles—and not come back until those troubles were cleared up. Then, to add to his emotional pain, the girl in his life dumped him.

Life in the pits

"I found myself at the bottom rung of life," Kevin says. "I got a day job, but the income only covered the minimum payments on my credit cards. I had to find a night job to take care of food and other living expenses."

That job, valet parking, required him to wear a uniform, including black Reebok tennis shoes he would have to buy for himself—at a cost of $50. With no money and maxed-out credit cards, $50 was an impossible sum, so Kevin went to a local discount store and found a pair of black ladies' gardening shoes for $5.99.

"I thought, man, this is so humiliating, but I could afford them," he says. "The problem was they had white bands around them, which my manager wouldn't allow. So, I took a black marker and covered up the bands. The marker wasn't permanent, so I had to keep it in my pocket. Whenever I scuffed the shoes and the white showed through, I had to paint them again so my manager wouldn't send me home."

A lesson in God's economics

One night, a local newscaster drove up in a Jaguar, and Kevin was assigned to park the car. He turned the radio dial and caught Larry Burkett on Crown's broadcast talking about money.

"Larry was talking about how God owns it all and how we are just stewards, managers, of what God entrusts to us," Kevin says. "He said most of us are poor managers, and I thought, *Man, I'm such a poor manager. I've mismanaged and mishandled everything He's given to me.*"

It struck him that he was driving a car that belonged to someone else. Even the bow tie on his neck belonged to the parking company. He didn't own anything but a pair of ladies' gardening shoes that he wasn't proud to claim.

He prayed, "God, if You could ever use a guy who's made so many mistakes—who's had to learn the hard way after You've given him so many chances—if You could use somebody like that, I'm Your man."

Applying the truth

Eager to learn what the Bible said about money, Kevin made numerous calls to Crown asking for every free item offered by the ministry. "If they had had caller ID in those days, they probably would have blocked my calls," he says. "From that day forward, I made a covenant with God to not only get out of debt and practice His financial principles but to surrender my heart to Him.

"Implementing the principles was very important, but the big victory was when I surrendered my heart, because then, God could do some great things through me."

Kevin began working to get out of debt, and eventually became a budget coach, hoping to steer other people away from the problems he'd experienced himself.

A new girl, Stephanie, came into his life, and he made a covenant with her not to be married until he had paid off all his debt. That didn't happen until four years later, on July 3, 1993, one month after he'd made the last payment on his student loan.

For the next four years, Kevin and Stephanie lived off his income and saved hers until they were able to make a 50 percent down payment on a house. In another four years they had completely paid off their mortgage.

By this time, Kevin had a bachelor's degree in accounting. He returned to school, earned a master's degree in taxation, and became an Enrolled Agent and Certified Public Accountant.

After 17 years of operating a CPA practice, he now devotes all of his time to speaking, teaching Crown seminars, and helping families as a Money Map Coach.

He jokes that most of the people he counsels haven't failed as much as he did. "It offers them great hope," he says. "They know they can definitely get out from where they are."

Your Response

So what do I do now?

We encourage you to write at least one Action Step in response to the chapter you have just read. If you write more than one, prioritize them in a logical order so you have a clear first step that you can begin immediately.

We also encourage you to reward yourself for every Action Step completed. Since the enemy ("the accuser") will discourage you by making the journey seem impossibly long, you need to see each step as its own victory. Your progress will be faster and more enjoyable if you take a little time to celebrate it.

Your celebration doesn't have to take a lot of time or money to be meaningful. Just make it something you enjoy, and tie it to the Action Step you have completed.

Action Steps

_____

_____

_____

_____

_____

_____

Celebration Plan

_____

_____

_____

_____

_____

_____

2
BANKRUPTCY

Bankruptcy is a serious matter and, at best, both sides lose.

Tears form in her eyes. In his, the anger of frustration gives way to resignation. After months of feeling trapped in a corner with no way out, his defensive crouch is reduced to a begging crawl. He is beaten.

One couple.

One set of circumstances.

Viewed in multiple ways by different people.

One counselor says, "You need to declare bankruptcy."

A friend says, "That's really tough. I wish I knew what to tell you," and hurries away, understandably uncomfortable facing such desperation with no easy fix.

Someone else says, "You're thinking of bankruptcy? Get thee behind me, Satan!" Well, they probably don't put it that way—at least to their face—but the couple can sense (or imagine) that response behind their backs.

Before we go any further, we want to make one thing very clear. We are on your side.

We say this because we know God is on your side. There is no other explanation for Calvary. God demonstrated that He was FOR us even though He condemned our sin. Regardless of how we measured up in comparison with someone else's level of sin, God righteously condemned all of us and then showed that He was still FOR us.

Ten of the most powerful words ever penned come from Paul when he raises this rhetorical question: *"If God is for us, who can be against us?"* (Romans 8:31, NIV). As you read the rest of this chapter, remember that we are FOR you and, more importantly, God is FOR you.

Bankruptcy is a delicate blend of justice and mercy. The fact that this legal remedy is sometimes abused does not mean that it should not exist, but we need to treat it with care.

Before we dig into the history and current legal specifics of bankruptcy, we want to reaffirm that we care about your unique circumstances and needs. We don't offer a one-size-fits-all solution. Instead, we educate you regarding what the law permits, what the consequences may be, and what alternatives you can consider. And, of course, we urge you to prayerfully seek knowledgeable counsel from a godly source.

The term **bankruptcy** comes from two Latin words meaning "bench" and "break," literally meaning "broken bench." Under Roman law, after gathering together and dividing up the assets of a delinquent debtor, the creditors would break the debtor's workbench as a punishment and a warning to other indebted tradesmen. Bankrupt individuals were regarded as thieves who deserved severe penalty. Romans deprived such persons of their civil rights, and many other societies stigmatized them by requiring them to dress in a particular identifying garb.

Revisions in contemporary bankruptcy laws have changed attitudes to the extent that consumers now regard it as a more plausible remedy for financial problems.

This trend spells great difficulty for many smaller merchants and for the credit industry as a whole. But, even more, it reflects a decline in the responsibility index for the average American family, Christian and non-Christian alike.

The dramatic increases in bankruptcy filings set the stage for another major revision: the Bankruptcy Abuse Prevention and Consumer Act of 2005. As the name implies, it attempts to curtail bankruptcy abuse by examining a debtor's ability to repay. Debtors who earn more than their state's median income may have their Chapter 7 cases disallowed if it is determined that they can repay a minimal amount of their unsecured debt over a five-year period.

The increased restrictions resulted in lower numbers of bankruptcy filings in 2006 and 2007, but they are rising again because of growing consumer debt and the home mortgage crisis.

Unfortunately, the credit card industry deliberately targets people who have just emerged from bankruptcy. Anticipating more profits from high interest rates, the industry knows its post-bankruptcy debtors cannot declare bankruptcy again for at least eight years.

Filing for Bankruptcy

Under all Chapters of bankruptcy the debtor must supply certain basic personal information (name, address, Social Security number), a list of all assets and all creditors to whom money is owed, and a form that shows the debtor's monthly income and monthly living expenses.

Depending on the Chapter selected, additional information may be required that is particular to that Chapter. Under Chapter 13, the debtor must file a proposed plan for payment to creditors within 10 days after the initial petition is filed.

An attorney should be consulted prior to filing under any Chapter.

The filing of any Chapter of bankruptcy temporarily stops all creditor collection efforts through an automatic stay. This automatic stay allows the debtor, and especially the trustee, to evaluate the debtor's condition and determine the best course of action concerning creditors. Creditors are placed in two basic categories: secured and unsecured.

Secured creditors have legal rights relating to any property pledged as collateral for the debt. The debtor must choose whether to surrender the collateral, reaffirm the debt, or redeem the collateral.

Unsecured creditors, such as credit cards, personal loans, and medical bills, do not have any rights to specific assets of the debtor and simply share in any distribution from the estate. Whether there is a distribution depends on the assets owned by the debtor and the exemption laws of the state in which the debtor resides.

Debts also are placed in two basic categories: dischargeable and non-dischargeable. Dischargeable debts, such as credit card debts, personal loans, and medical bills, are the category forgiven by the Bankruptcy Code. Non-dischargeable debts, which must be repaid, include student loans, alimony and child support, and most taxes. Certain debts that otherwise would be classified as dischargeable may be reclassified as non-dischargeable if the debt was created through fraud or misrepresentation on the part of the debtor.

Bankruptcy Chapters

Bankruptcy laws and procedures are much too complicated to cover in this book, and individual circumstances can affect the choice of which bankruptcy chapter to select. We will provide here only a simple overview of the various Chapters of the Bankruptcy Code. *Specific advice should be sought from a qualified attorney.* The following Chapters of bankruptcy are presented in the order in which they are most frequently filed.

> **Chapter 7**—This Chapter covers the majority of all bankruptcies—both personal and business.

A trustee is immediately appointed to administer the bankruptcy proceedings. In most cases the debtor will never see the judge and will deal only with the appointed trustee.

The function of Chapter 7 is to liquidate all nonexempt assets and distribute the proceeds to creditors based on the proof of claim filed by the creditor and allowed by the trustee. Most creditors receive only a small percentage of the original outstanding debts.

Debtors are allowed to keep items that are specified as exempt. As long as they are honest in dealing with the trustee and do not withhold any nonexempt assets, the court grants a discharge: the formal forgiveness of all remaining debt.

> **Chapter 13**—This Chapter affords personal debtors an opportunity to repay their creditors, based on the ability to pay. The majority of Chapter 13 cases are filed by individuals facing a foreclosure against their homes, since Chapter 13 will allow them to make back payments and reinstate their mortgages.

Chapter 13 has very specific limits regarding the amount and type of debt it will cover. It is not available to corporations.

Under Chapter 13 a trustee is immediately appointed to administer the case and review the initial schedules filed along with the proposed plan for payment to creditors. The debtor pays the trustee the amount specified in the plan each month, and the trustee pays the bills and deals with all the creditors. The proposed plan may provide for distributions of payments to creditors for a period of time, not to exceed 60 months. It could be a shorter period, depending on the debtor's ability to pay as determined by the trustee. On the successful completion of the payment plan, the court formally discharges (forgives) any remaining balance due to creditors.

Don't Do It Alone

If these bankruptcy specifics seem confusing or overwhelming, remember that these are not actions to be taken alone. Your attorney will walk you through the process. Make sure to ask questions about anything you don't understand, including the ethical implications of a proposed plan.

Also remember that God is not absent in this process. He is all about new beginnings. After David's recognition of his sin with Bathsheba, he brokenheartedly repented. Psalm 51 allows us to enter into the depth of his honest regret. He didn't have any illusions about escaping the consequences of his sin, but he did have confidence that God would not reject him. *"The sacrifices of God are a broken spirit; a broken and contrite heart, O God, you will not despise"* (Psalm 51:17).

Whether you are baffled about why He has allowed your circumstances or you recognize them as consequences of your own actions, you can be sure that God has not abandoned you. Nor does He have sweaty palms regarding your future. His primary concern is that *"all things work together for good"* (Romans 8:28) in the process of conforming you to the image of His Son (Romans 8:29; 12:2).

> **Chapter 11**—This Chapter, although available to individuals, is most frequently filed by corporations. Chapter 11 permits a company to continue operating its business under the supervision of the Bankruptcy Court for up to four months while formulating a repayment plan.

Any proposed plan must pay creditors at least the amount they would receive if the company were immediately liquidated under Chapter 7. After the plan is submitted, the creditors vote to decide whether to liquidate the corporation or allow it to reorganize under the plan.

> **Chapter 12**—The Frazier-Lemke Act of 1933 gave farmers special consideration under Section 75 of the Bankruptcy Act. It stipulated that a farmer could not be the subject of an involuntary petition (creditor-initiated liquidation).

Because of the unique particulars of a Chapter 12 case, a qualified attorney should be consulted.

> **Chapter 15**—This Chapter was added in 2005 for business bankruptcies involving more than one country.
>
> *Bankruptcy laws are continually changing so please consult an attorney or CPA before you make any decisions*

Is Bankruptcy Unscriptural?

This is not a simple question to answer. God's Word clearly says that believers should be responsible for their promises and repay what they owe. *"When you make a vow to God, do not be late in paying it; for He takes no delight in fools. Pay what you vow! It is better that you should not vow than that you should vow and not pay"* (Ecclesiastes 5:4-5).

Does that mean that in the interim you should not take the legal remedy of court protection until you have the ability to repay? Often that will be an individual decision. First and foremost, a Christian must be willing to accept the absolute requirement to repay every debt.

Next, the issue of motive must be addressed. Is the bankruptcy action being taken to protect the legitimate rights of the creditors? The answer to this question can be found in whether assets are purposely withheld from the creditors. For example, many people who file for corporate or personal bankruptcy protection have already unfairly shielded assets by transferring them to a spouse or other family members.

If a debtor's intent is merely to retain assets without due consideration of the creditors, the action is unscriptural. It would be better to suffer the loss of all assets than to lose your integrity. *"Do not withhold good from those to whom it is due, when it is in your power to do it. Do not say to your neighbor, 'Go, and come back, and tomorrow I will give it,' when you have it with you"* (Proverbs 3:27-28).

Bankruptcy is a serious matter and, at best, both sides lose. The creditors lose much of the money they are owed, and debtors lose some of the respect they previously had. There is still a stigma associated with any bankruptcy, and it will remain until the last creditor is repaid.

There Is More Than One Option

People who despair of ever getting free of their debt are tempted to think that bankruptcy is their only reasonable option. Often, this is not the case. Crown Money Map Coaches have helped many people formulate a plan that avoids bankruptcy and still meets their needs.

Those who have already filed for bankruptcy can turn an otherwise negative situation into a positive one by making a commitment to repay what they legitimately owe. Once that commitment is made, they can look to God to provide the means to follow through.

Questions and Answers

If I file for bankruptcy protection, what happens to debts cosigned by friends or relatives?

Any cosigners are still liable to pay whatever portion of the debt is unpaid.

Can I avoid the IRS through a bankruptcy?

Many people have the mistaken impression that filing for bankruptcy voids an obligation to the Internal Revenue Service. Not so. The Bankruptcy Code excludes several categories of debt from the set-aside provisions of the law (non-dischargeable debts), including most federal and state income tax liabilities. Also excluded are federally backed school loans.

Should I file for bankruptcy because of a large lawsuit judgment?

It is possible to be sued for millions of dollars over an accident. In light of this, prudent people carry appropriate amounts of liability insurance. However, in the face of an unreasonable judgment in which damages are clearly punitive rather than compensatory, filing for protection may be an option to prayerfully consider.

What is the difference between a "straight" bankruptcy and a Chapter 13 plan?

> A CHRISTIAN MUST BE WILLING TO ACCEPT THE ABSOLUTE REQUIREMENT TO REPAY EVERY DEBT.

Straight bankruptcy (Chapter 7) is a legal way to make most debts disappear with no legal requirement to repay them. A Chapter 13 plan provides a systematic way to repay most, if not all, debts under court supervision and protection.

What will Chapter 13 repayment proceedings do to my credit rating?

Credit reporting agencies currently report the filing of any bankruptcy for a period of 10 years. In a Chapter 13 filing, the reporting includes the amount of the debts owed, the amount of the repayment to creditors, and whether the debtor successfully completed the plan.

Will I lose my job if I go through bankruptcy?

Employers are forbidden to fire an employee because of bankruptcy proceedings. However, certain jobs in which the employee must be bonded (such as a jewelry clerk or bank teller) may be jeopardized.

Am I obligated to repay if my creditors force me into bankruptcy?

This is a situation in which many people feel justified in not repaying their debts because they did not choose bankruptcy; their creditors did. However, Psalm 37:21 says, *"The wicked borrows and does not pay back, but the righteous is gracious and gives."* God's Word is clear: You are obligated to repay what you borrow.

Remember that when God obligates you to do something, it is always for your good. And He will reward your faithful obedience with the needed resources to follow through.

Additionally, your credit rating can be restored by repaying all debts. Be sure the credit bureau's files reflect your changed status. (A letter from your creditors verifying that all debts have been paid is very helpful.)

From Bankruptcy to Blessing
The Story of Phil Drake

As a young man with an interest in technology and an entrepreneurial spirit, Phil Drake began automating his father's accounting practice with one of IBM's earliest computers in 1976. He created tax processing programs for the new computer, and when the IBM salesman made a follow-up visit, he asked Phil to travel with him and sell his software.

Shock and surrender

"I was a Christian, but my mentality in those days was that God helps those who help themselves. I thought I was supposed to do everything on my own and call on God only when I got into trouble. I told Sharon I would be a millionaire by age 30, but God chose that age for me to be bankrupt.

"We had grown too fast and added employees, and we owed a lot of payroll taxes. The IRS closed our business in 1981, and we ended up in Chapter 11 bankruptcy. Our debt was six times our annual gross income, and the bankruptcy court determined we had the ability to pay only 20 percent of our debt."

Since the late 1970s, Phil had been listening to Larry Burkett on Crown's broadcast over WLFJ in Greenville, South Carolina. He'd heard Larry talk about paying back 100 percent after a bankruptcy, and he and Sharon decided they wanted to honor the Lord by repaying everything they owed—however long it took.

"I told God I had messed up, and I started relying on Him," Phil says. "We paid off all our debts by 1987, only six years later. And since the bankruptcy, God has blessed what we've done."

A harvest of blessings

Today, Drake Software serves tax preparers all over the country. It was involved in the processing of millions of federal and state returns.

But God's blessings on Phil have gone far beyond his software company, which employs about 350 people. Currently, he operates about a dozen businesses in Macon County, North Carolina, including a Christian bookstore and a Christian radio station.

The last business he opened is a family entertainment center called "The Factory." It's housed in a former Burlington Industries sewing plant where his mother worked in the 1950s.

All of his three children are Christians, and he now has the privilege of being a spiritual mentor for his grandchildren.

But Phil sees his responsibility to influence others as going beyond his family, and the bookstore, radio station, and entertainment center are part of his efforts to influence the culture in Franklin.

Beyond his hometown, Phil is supporting organizations like Crown, Family Research Council, Compassion International, and Focus on the Family, which have means to influence the culture in other places.

"When I get to heaven, God won't ask me how much money I made. He'll ask me how I used the money and who I brought with me. I want to bring people with me, and to do that, I have to be a good steward."

Action Steps

_____

_____

_____

_____

_____

Celebration Plan

_____

_____

_____

_____

_____

CHAPTER

3 GAMBLING & LOTTERIES

In today's culture gambling is creating a series of unintended consequences.

Why a Chapter on Gambling?

Debt and bankruptcy are both serious problems with multiple causes. For a growing number of families, one of those causes is gambling.

Although gambling has probably been around since the entrance of sin into the world, its increasing presence in today's culture is creating a series of unanticipated consequences.

More importantly, the Bible speaks to the issue. It is not as direct as "Thou shalt not gamble," but a reasonable examination of multiple Scriptures will demonstrate that gambling sabotages God's purpose for us. And remember that His purpose and our welfare are always connected.

What Is Gambling?

Webster defines it as "playing a game for money." This innocent-sounding definition hides several awful realities.

- The risk of loss is at least as great as the opportunity to gain—usually greater.
- Human nature causes gamblers to consistently lose winnings and walk away with losses.
- Gambling creates no value other than entertainment that costs more than anticipated.
- Gambling's addictive nature destroys many families.

Alarming Growth

The number of casinos around the country continues to grow because of their extreme profitability.

That alone is cause for concern, but it is compounded by the fact that the majority of states plus the District of Columbia now sponsor and promote legalized gambling in the form of lotteries.

Rather than protecting the poor—an expected function of government—state lotteries contribute to the desperation of the poor.

Astronomical Odds

The poor tend to be greater victims of the lottery simply by virtue of the fact that they have smaller incomes. "For the poor, the lottery is not 'harmless entertainment,'" says Dr. J. Emmett Henderson, head of the Georgia Council on Moral and Civic Concerns. "It is a desperate but vain attempt to survive. But odds of winning are so cruel that lotteries turn out to be theft by consent."

Even for people in higher income groups, the lottery is still a rip-off. "The odds of winning are so astronomical that no state can run a successful lottery and tell its people the truth," Henderson says.

In one California lotto, the odds of winning were one in 23 million. Henderson says the immensity of these odds can be illustrated by a line of dollar bills placed end to end from Georgia all the way to the Golden Gate Bridge in California. Out of all those dollar bills, the winner would have to pick the one with a certain serial number.

Unfortunately, some people believe that, with the help of "magic" or "luck," they can beat these astronomical odds.

"I visited New Hampshire, the first lottery state in modern times," says Henderson. "I found that the government-run lottery attracts and stimulates an industry of astrologers, soothsayers, psychics, numerologists, fortune tellers, and seers. All these pseudo-religious charlatans ride piggyback on government lottery. For a price they claim they can make you rich by helping you divine the winning lottery number."

A study by Sandeep Mangalmurti and Robert Allan Cooke, PhD, (*State Lotteries: Seducing the Less Fortunate?* published by the Heartland Institute of Chicago) exposes many concerns, including that of lottery officials manipulating people's superstitions about winning the lottery. "Many states," they say, "perpetuate the myth of 'winning methods' and the contradictory fallacies of numbers being 'hot' because they have been picked often or 'due' because they have not been picked recently."

Breeding New Addicts

The most devastating effect of lotteries is that they make it easier for nongamblers to start gambling. One out of 10 adults who gamble will become addicted.

"A lottery is to gambling addiction what marijuana is to drug addiction," Henderson says. "The lottery is the gateway. Research across the country shows that the number of compulsive gamblers addicted to lotteries significantly escalates once a lottery is in operation."

The fact that a state puts its "okay" on the lottery helps people lay aside their reservations about playing. And if someone wants to spend money on a lottery ticket, chances are he or she won't have to drive far to buy one.

"If lottery tickets are anything, they are widely available," say Mangal-murti and Cooke. "They can be purchased at virtually any convenience store, through the mail, and over the phone."

Not surprisingly, the availability of lotteries is often accompanied by a higher level of juvenile problems, according to the National Council on Compulsive Gambling in New York. And more teenagers are likely to gamble in states where a lottery is available.

Odds Chart

The odds of winning a lotto jackpot are roughly **13 million to one.** *But as shown, you're more likely to see a no-hitter, find a pearl in an oyster, or be struck by lightning.*

Seeing a no-hitter
1 in 1,347

Finding a pearl in an oyster
1 in 12,000

Being dealt a royal flush in 5-card stud
1 in 649,739

Having quadruplets
1 in 705,000

Being struck by lightning
1 in 1,900,000

For example, after a lottery was introduced in California, the percentage of students who were gambling rose from 22 to 40 percent. In Virginia, it rose from 26 to 58 percent.

Gambling addiction can be a terrible experience for teenagers and for their parents. "Any parent who thinks gambling isn't as bad as drinking or drugs is dreaming," says the father of a teenage addicted gambler. "As a parent, I can tell you it's a real nightmare."

Teens addicted to gambling are future employees. And along with adult compulsive gamblers, they are bad news for businesses.

"Like alcoholism and drug addiction, compulsive gambling is costly to the economy," Henderson says. "In fact, most of the dysfunctional consequences of gambling addiction are job related. These include lowered productivity, use of work time to gamble, absenteeism, high rates of business failure, and repeated nonpayment of loans, mortgages, and other financial obligations."

The American Insurance Institute estimates that as much as 40 percent of America's white collar crime is committed by compulsive gamblers. This problem can be expected to grow, considering the rampant growth of gambling.

According to John Kindt, a professor at the University of Illinois, for every dollar we receive from taxes on gambling, three dollars is needed for such things as increased police protection and treating gambling addicts.

Why Gamble?

"Lotteries express the age-old fantasy of acquiring wealth painlessly, without effort or labor," Henderson says. "Common sense tells us life does not function that way. No state can turn its back on initiative and hard work and expect its economy to prosper. Wage earners cannot buy lottery tickets and, at the same time, maintain the same level of purchasing food, clothing, and other marketplace commodities.

"A wholesome and prosperous society is one that is built on hard work, creativity, thrift, and government integrity. State lottery undermines the work ethic, hurts the economy, and adds to the unemployment statistics and welfare rolls. Its promotion by government is nothing but another siren song luring the nation toward the rocks of economic ruin."

When Henderson says, "Lotteries express the age-old fantasy of acquiring wealth painlessly, without effort or labor," he exposes one of the central motivations for why people gamble.

Many of them, having trouble meeting their needs through earned income perceive gambling as their "opportunity" to acquire material comforts. These are the people who used to play the $2 window at the race track. Today, they play their state lottery.

Another group gambles just for the fun of it. They say it doesn't matter if they win or lose. But let them start winning and you'll find out that's not so.

These are "social" gamblers. They go on vacation with a set amount of money. Once it's gone, they pack up and go home, often living conservative lives that require disciplined budgeting.

The last group gambles compulsively. To them, gambling is a disease that wrecks their finances, families, and careers. The compulsive gamblers will lie, steal, cheat, and use virtually everyone around them.

A game of chance is to them what alcohol is to the alcoholic. Often, they are successful professionals with promising careers. For example, one compulsive gambler maintained a successful career for several years while flying to Las Vegas twice a month without his wife even knowing about it. His dual life ended with his owing over $200,000 in gambling debts to underworld leaders.

At first glance, each of these types of gamblers would appear to have different motives for gambling but, in reality, they all suffer from the same basic problem: materialism. The one who gambles when in need is looking for the "big hit" just like the social gambler or the compulsive gambler.

A Biblical Perspective

"In all labor there is profit, but mere talk leads only to poverty" (Proverbs 14:23).

Gambling may be considered labor for a pit boss in Vegas, but for gamblers, it's a scheme to escape labor—at least in most cases. It is the ultimate get-rich-quick scheme, satisfying every element of the get-rich-quick philosophy.

- Participants are encouraged to risk money they usually can't afford to lose.

- They know little or nothing about what they're doing.

- They're forced to make hasty decisions.

- The whole idea is to operate on the "greater sucker" theory. In other words, when you dump money into the slot machine, you believe there was a greater sucker who risked his or her money and then quit just before the big jackpot.

Get-rich-quick schemes frequently target the weak and naïve. Gambling is an almost irresistible enticement to people who desire to meet the wants and needs of their families but find that they cannot. That's why state lotteries have become so popular.

But Is Gambling a Sin?

Gambling is enticing someone to gain money at the certain loss of another. It breeds and even promotes selfishness, greed, and covetousness. The Apostle Paul warned against this earthly kind of mindset when he said, *"Many walk, of whom I often told you, and now tell you even weeping, that they are enemies of the cross of Christ, whose end is destruction, whose god is their appetite, and whose glory is in their shame, who set their minds on earthly things"* (Philippians 3:18-19).

Regardless of how socially acceptable the practice of gambling has become, it's still preying upon the weaknesses of others. This runs counter to the Scriptures, which encourage us to help the weak and seek good for all men.

"We urge you, brethren, admonish the unruly, encourage the faint-hearted, help the weak, be patient with everyone. See that no one repays another with evil for evil, but always seek after that which is good for one another and for all people" (1 Thessalonians 5:14-15).

Paul frequently reminds us to live by a higher standard than that of the world (Romans 12:2). In conjunction with this, we shouldn't do anything that would give cause for offense or that might discredit our witness (2 Corinthians 6:3).

Even if a Christian believes he or she is free to gamble, it is likely to cause others to stumble. We're clearly directed in 1 Corinthians 8:13 to avoid anything that would cause a weaker Christian to stumble.

No Longer Hiding
Brenda Kay's Story

I always enjoyed playing poker with my family and friends. After my husband and I were married, we played poker with some other couples. That was fun, and winning was really exciting! But gambling moved beyond fun when I was introduced to a casino and slot machines. Our family was having some difficulties, so my husband and I wanted to get away for a few days.

It was a riverboat casino with winding stairs, big chandeliers, a bar and the whole works. I told my husband that I felt like Scarlett O'Hara!

After losing several rolls of quarters, we decided to play nickel machines. We sat together playing those machines for hours, and we had a ball! It was so much fun to hit jackpots and have coins falling all over us. We enjoyed the excitement of winning, the lights, the sounds and being together. It was a wonderful weekend!

I couldn't wait to go back, so I rolled nickels and quarters to get ready. We had been playing progressive slots, so I was all set to win a million dollars on the slots! We didn't go to the casino too often. In those days, I played bingo a lot during the day, but I realized that I could drive an hour-and-a-half to the casino and have a lot more fun. One day, as soon as my husband left for work, I got dressed and drove to the casino. I made sure to get back before my husband got home from work.

The first few times, I took $50 to $100, but soon, that wasn't enough. I saved every way I could so I could take $200 or more. I never came home with any money. If I won a jackpot, I stayed until all of it was gone. To get enough money to gamble, I stopped paying our bills. I stole my husband's Post Office box key so he couldn't check the mail and see the bills. I took the phone off the hook at night so bill collectors couldn't call, and I stole the tape out of the telephone answering machine. I hid all the bills and overdue notices in shoeboxes in the closet.

After several months of hiding all this from my husband, we were six months behind on our house note, and we had three or four maxed out credit cards. We owed everybody. I took $200 for the light bill to the casino planning to make enough money to pay off a lot of our debts, but of course, that never happened. One day on the way back from the casino, I hit bottom. I had ruined our lives. I thought, "If I just pull out in front of an 18-wheeler, I'll die and my husband will have the life insurance money. That'll fix everything." I just wanted to die.

I wrote a note to a friend at church to borrow some money, but she gave it to my pastor. He called me and asked me to see him. He confronted me, and I was so ashamed. I told him what I'd been doing, and he told me to go home and tell my husband. I would rather die, but I decided to tell him. I hated myself for making such a mess of our lives. I wanted my husband—or somebody—to hit me because I deserved to be in pain. My husband asked his brother for advice, and he called the number on the back of a lottery ticket to find some help. We found a Gamblers Anonymous meeting, and he drove me to my first meeting.

It was so hard to stop gambling. For the first few months in the group, I cried because I felt so ashamed. I told them about all the hot checks and hiding bills, and at the end of the meetings, they hugged me and told me how proud they were of me. That was incredible.

Even from the beginning of my recovery, God worked in powerful ways, and He helped me restore our marriage. We had some tough times. I was miserable giving up gambling, and I wanted my husband to be miserable, too. But God got us through it all. Today, I'm happier than I've ever been.

Compulsive Gambling

Compulsive gamblers are as much addicted to risk taking as a drug addict is to drugs. It stands to reason that the number of compulsive gamblers will grow as gambling becomes more and more accessible to people in every state.

Sometimes, compulsive gamblers are church members who are supported in part through a church benevolence fund. Fund administrators may be unaware that the "needs" of this member are more than food, clothing, and shelter.

Churches can avoid being "taken" if they will require counseling for any benevolence fund recipient. In addition, they must require that both husband and wife attend counseling sessions. Common characteristics for counselors to look for in compulsive gamblers:

1. an unusually high debt load with little or no logical explanation for it;

2. a history of borrowing from virtually every friend and family member; and

3. a vehement denial of anything to do with gambling.

Only in response to a direct question about gambling is a spouse likely to reveal the truth. A compulsive gambler may hide it from the outside world but, eventually, his or her spouse will find out.

Gamblers need love and acceptance, but it must be accompanied by accountability. They need to be held accountable to pay their debts, tell the truth, and stay away from all gambling. If God's people don't hold to this same standard, it becomes difficult to give good counsel to a compulsive gambler.

Deception

Satan, the master deceiver and father of lies, is successfully duping our culture into believing that legalized gambling will lower taxes without promoting crime and family dysfunction.

Many Christians buy this lie and support lotteries, bingo, or racing—all under the assumption that gambling doesn't really hurt anyone.

Is this the type of environment we want for our children? If not, we must remember that we pass our value system, including our views about gambling, along to those around us: first to our own families, then to our friends and neighbors. If our value system is no better than the value system of the world in which we live, truly we have been conformed to the "image" of this world.

"Whether, then, you eat or drink or whatever you do, do all to the glory of God. Give no offense either to Jews or to Greeks or to the church of God; just as I also please all men in all things, not seeking my own profit but the profit of the many, so that they may be saved" (1 Corinthians 10:31-33).

God Is the Source of Power

We have attempted to paint a realistic picture of the growing problem of gambling. Although we need to recognize its deception and take it seriously, we want to make sure that we focus on God's power to deliver us from this or any other bondage.

God wants us to be free from bondage, free to serve Him in love and gratitude. He is a deliverer for those who wholeheartedly trust and obey Him. Remember these four powerful truths.

1. He has a vested interest in our freedom since He gave His only Son as its price. *"...He has died as a ransom to set them free..."* (Hebrews 9:15, NIV).

2. He will provide an avenue of escape. *"No temptation has seized you except what is common to man. And God is faithful; he will not let you be tempted beyond what you can bear. But when you are tempted, he will also provide a way out so that you can stand up under it"* (1 Corinthians 10:13, NIV).

3. We can look to Him with confidence. *"If the Son sets you free, you will be free indeed"* (John 8:36, NIV).

4. Nothing can overpower Him. *"Greater is He who is in you than he who is in the world"* (1 John 4:4).

What You Can Do

If you are not tempted to gamble, thank God for one less booby-trap in your path. You can:

- decide never to support any form of gambling;

- vote against all gambling initiatives and those who support them;

- teach your children about its dangers; and

- don't hide your convictions. You can be open without being condescending or judgmental.

If, on the other hand, you wrestle with the temptation, don't ignore it. Satan will provide an endless supply of rationalizations—that is his profession. Instead, you can:

- Confess your desire to God. It will not surprise Him. His help awaits your invitation.

- Recognize that deliverance and healing from any addiction are usually processes in which you are required to participate. Don't expect a simple gift or zap. Sometimes, however, just a glimpse from God's perspective can be so powerful that it makes all the difference as it

  o reveals how damaging your actions are to those you love and

  o reveals who you are in His sight so that you are no longer willing to live below your calling.

- Seek the counsel of your pastor or trusted friend.

- Seek professional help. Among those we recommend:

  o Residential Treatment for Compulsive Gamblers - http://www.lostbet.com/   1-800-567-8238

  o http://www.gamblersanonymous.org

  o www.troubledwith.com - Look for gambling articles under Abuse/ Addiction. This Web site is by Focus on the Family.

  o www.ncpgambling.org - National Council on Problem Gambling. You can search for a nationally certified counselor online.

  o 24-hour confidential helpline - 1-800-522-4700

- Find (or start, if necessary) a support and accountability group.

Action Steps

_____

_____

_____

_____

_____

_____

Celebration Plan

_____

_____

_____

_____

CHAPTER 4
WRAPPING IT UP WITH HOPE

Just in case you're struggling with one or more of the problems we've discussed so far, we want to take a moment to assure you of several things.

- **God is not shocked by your failures.** *"As for you, you were dead in your transgressions and sins, in which you used to live when you followed the ways of this world and of the ruler of the kingdom of the air, the spirit who is now at work in those who are disobedient. All of us also lived among them at one time, gratifying the cravings of our sinful nature and following its desires and thoughts. Like the rest, we were by nature objects of wrath"* (Ephesians 2:1-3, NIV).

- **God's love for you is unconditional and constant.** It is not dependent on your ability to perform up to some standard—yours or anyone else's. *"But because of his great love for us, God, who is rich in mercy, made us alive with Christ even when we were dead in transgressions—it is by grace you have been saved. And God raised us up with Christ and seated us with him in the heavenly realms in Christ Jesus, in order that in the coming ages he might show the incomparable riches of his grace, expressed in his kindness to us in Christ Jesus. For it is by grace you have been saved, through faith—and this not from yourselves, it is the gift of God—not by works, so that no one can boast"* Ephesians 2:4-9, NIV).

- **God's Spirit convicts us of sin—not to condemn but to call us to repentance.** Hiding from it is impossible. Running from it does no good. Responding to it results in huge relief and the joy of reconciliation. *"If we claim to be without sin, we deceive ourselves and the truth is not in us. If we confess our sins, he is faithful and just and will forgive us our sins and purify us from all unrighteousness"* (1 John 1:8-9, NIV).

- **You are not alone in your struggle.** *"No temptation has seized you except what is common to man. And God is faithful; he will not let you be tempted beyond what you can bear. But when you are tempted, he will also provide a way out so that you can stand up under it"* (1 Corinthians 10:13, NIV).

- **God has a better plan for you.** *"For I know the plans I have for you," declares the LORD, "plans to prosper you and not to harm you, plans to give you hope and a future. Then you will call upon me and come and pray to me, and I will listen to you. You will seek me and find me when you seek me with all your heart"* (Jeremiah 29:11-13, NIV).

- **If you have surrendered your life to Christ, you are part of His body.** This means that you are loved and valued by others in the body. *"Now you are the body of Christ, and each one of you is a part of it"* (1 Corinthians 12:27, NIV). First Corinthians 12 describes how God has gifted people with differing abilities so that together we can help each other to wholeness.

Here's an all-important question for you: Can you fully accept God's unconditional love and forgiveness? You cannot say yes to that and fail to forgive yourself. Is your standard superior to His? Do you think He forgives you so that you can remain in bondage to yourself?

Accepting God's forgiveness means that your chains of guilt have been removed regardless of what consequences you may still bear for past actions. You have been freed from self-imposed separation from Him. Failing to live in that freedom is failing to accept His forgiveness.

God wants you to live fully forgiven. He did not pay the awful price of His Son's sacrifice in the hope that you would refuse it. Gratefully accept it—fully!

Action Steps

_____

_____

_____

_____

_____

Celebration Plan

_____

_____

_____

_____

_____

SECTION TWO

SPENDING PLAN SOLUTIONS

Stuck?

It happens all the time. Somewhere, right now, someone is getting stuck. Sometimes people don't see the flooded dip in the road as they approach it. Sometimes they see it and think it's not deep enough to stop them. Or that if it does, they can just float for a bit while it goes down.

Some manage to plow through it and assume they can do the same with the next one. Others get hung up and need to be bailed out before resuming their journey. Still others hydroplane off the road or into the path of oncoming traffic. Some barely escape with their lives. Some don't.

You know we're not really talking about flash floods and cars, right? Mismanaged finances and their accompanying stress can be just as dangerous as a flash flood.

We don't want to be melodramatic; we just want to underscore the point. How we handle money has serious implications. Most of us need solutions, a plan that is better than our present habits.

SPENDING PLAN/ BUDGETING

Comprehensive help for putting it all together

It seems to be a natural law of economics: Regardless of how much our income increases, our expenses manage to consume it. And then some.

Our checking accounts often resemble the formula for water; instead of two parts hydrogen for one part oxygen, substitute two parts expenses for one part income. The solution, of course, is to create a spending plan and live by it.

Many people just shoot from the hip, hoping everything will turn out okay, because taking time to track the numbers doesn't seem very enjoyable at first. Many of us don't particularly enjoy brushing our teeth, either, but we've learned that the discipline beats the alternative—by a long shot.

> **Bad news:** Creating a spending plan will take some time and effort.
>
> **Good news:** It will be customized to meet your needs.
>
> **Better news:** It will save lots of time and effort in years to come.
>
> **Best news:** It will pay off for the rest of your life.

Rather than being an inflexible straitjacket, a spending plan delivers surprising freedom. It removes mystery, fear and the exhaustion of struggling to keep our noses above the water line of debt.

Steps to Create a Spending Plan

Creating a spending plan that fits you perfectly is the goal for this chapter. We'll follow several logical steps in the process. We'll also provide helpful forms in two versions, one with with sample numbers plugged in for illustration and one with blanks to fill in.

Step 1—List Monthly Household Expenditures.

a. Fixed Expenses

- Tithe
- Federal income taxes (if taxes are deducted, ignore this item)
- State income taxes (if taxes are deducted, ignore this item)
- Federal Social Security taxes (if taxes are deducted, ignore this item)
- Housing expenses (payment/rent)
- Residence (Real Estate) taxes
- Residence insurance
- Other

b. Variable Expenses

- Food
- Outstanding debts
- Utilities
- Insurance (life, health, auto)
- Entertainment/recreation
- Clothing allowance
- Medical/dental
- Savings/miscellaneous

NOTE: In order to accurately determine variable expenses, both husband and wife should keep an expense diary for 30 days. Every expenditure, even small purchases, should be listed.

Step 2—List Available Monthly Income.

NOTE: If your income varies from month to month, use a yearly average divided by 12 to establish a monthly average.

- Salary
- Rents
- Interest
- Dividends
- Income tax refund
- Notes (loans you have made to others that they are

repaying you)
- Other

Step 3—Compare Income Versus Expenses.

We encourage couples to base their spending plan, as much as possible, on one spouse's income—thereby reducing the family's vulnerability to lost income due to illness, pregnancy, or a change in employment location. The other spouse's income can be allocated to one-time purchases—vacations, furniture, cars—or to savings, debt reduction or giving.

If you are in the fortunate position of having total income that exceeds total expenses, your spending plan's primary role will be to speed your progress towards the ultimate goal of financial faithfulness—including the ability to serve in any way God directs without the need of a salary.

If, however, your expenses exceed income (or you simply desire more stringent controls in spending), you will need to analyze each spending plan category to reduce expenses. These categories are outlined below along with some guidance for the percentage of your income they will probably require.

"Budget busters" are the large potential problem areas that routinely ruin a spending plan. Failure to control even one of these problems can result in a family financial disaster.

The percentage of net income we suggest for each category is based on successful spending plans for families of four with a $45,000 annual income. These percentages are not absolutes and will vary with income and geographic location.

a. Housing (32 percent of net income)

Typically, this is one of the largest spending plan problems. Many families buy homes they can't afford. The decision to buy or rent should be based on needs and financial ability rather than on peer pressure or an unrealistic expectation of gain.

b. Food (13 percent of net income)

Many families buy too much food. Others buy too little. The average American family tends to buy the wrong type of food. The reduction of a family's food bill requires quantity and quality planning.

Hints for Grocery Shopping

- Always use a written list of needs.

- Try to conserve gas by buying food for a longer time period and in larger quantities.

- Avoid buying when hungry.

- Use a calculator, if possible, to keep a running subtotal.

- Reduce or eliminate paper products—paper plates, cups, napkins (use cloth napkins).

- Evaluate where to purchase sundry items, such as shampoo, mouthwash. (These are usually less expensive at discount stores.)

- Avoid processed and sugar-coated cereals. (These are expensive and most of them have little nutritional value.)

- Avoid prepared foods, such as frozen dinners, pot pies, cakes. (You are paying for expensive labor that you can provide.)

- Determine good meat cuts that are available from roasts or shoulders, and have the butcher cut these for you. (Buying steaks by the package on sale is fairly inexpensive also.)

- Try store brand canned products. (These are normally cheaper and just as nutritious.)

- Avoid products in a seasonal price hike. Substitute or eliminate.

- Shop for advertised specials. (These are usually posted in the store window.)

- Use manufacturer's coupons (cents-off on an item or items) only if you were going to buy the item anyway and it is cheaper than another brand without the coupon.

- When possible, purchase food in bulk quantities from large discount stores; the per-item cost is cheaper. Do not buy from convenience stores except in case of emergency.

- Avoid buying non-grocery items in a grocery supermarket except on sale. (These are normally "high mark-up" items.)

- For baby foods, use normal foods processed in a blender.

- If possible, leave children at home with a responsible adult to avoid unnecessary pressure.

- Check every item as it is being "rung up" at the store and again when you get home.

- Consider canning fresh vegetables whenever possible. Make bulk purchases with other families at farmers' markets or wherever you can get the best value. (NOTE: Buy canning supplies during off seasons.)

c. Transportation (13 percent of net income)

The advertising media refers to us as "consumers," but that's not always the best description. P.T. Barnum had a more apt word— "suckers." Often we are unwise in our decision making when it comes to machines—especially cars.

Many families will buy new cars they cannot afford and trade them much sooner than necessary. Those who buy a new car, keeping it for less than four years and then trading it for another new car, waste the maximum amount of money. Some people, such as salespeople who drive a great deal, need new cars frequently; most of us do not. We swap cars because we want to—not because we have to.

d. Insurance (5 percent of net income)

Few people understand insurance, resulting in poor decisions and lost money. Some buy high-cost insurance they don't need and can't afford; others have none, exposing themselves to unacceptable risk. It is important to know what kind and how much is needed.

Insurance should be used as supplementary provision for the family, not for profit. An insurance plan is not designed for saving money or for retirement. Ask anyone who assumed it was; the ultimate result was disillusionment.

One of your best insurance assets is to have a trustworthy agent who will create a simple plan to analyze your exact needs. Independent agents can select from several different companies to provide you with the best possible options.

e. Debts (5 percent of net income)

It would be great if most budgets included 5 percent debts or less. Unfortunately, the norm in American families is far in excess of this amount because of the proliferation of credit cards, bank loans, and installment credit. What can you do once this situation exists?

- Destroy all credit cards as a first step.

- Establish a payment schedule that includes all creditors.

- Contact all creditors, honestly relate your problems, and arrange an equitable repayment plan.

- Buy on a cash basis, and sacrifice your wants and desires until you are current.

f. Entertainment/Recreation (5 percent of net income)

We are a recreation-oriented culture. That is not necessarily bad if put in the proper perspective. But those who are in debt cannot use their creditor's money to entertain themselves. The normal tendency is to escape pain for the moment—even if the problems then become more acute. We must resist this urge and control recreation and entertainment expenses while in debt.

What a terrible witness it is for a follower of Christ who is in financial bondage to indulge at the expense of others. God knows we need rest and relaxation; once our attitude is correct, He will often provide it from unexpected sources. Every believer, whether in debt or not, should seek to reduce entertainment expenses. This usually can be done without sacrificing quality family time.

Recreation Hints

- Plan vacations during "off seasons" if possible.

- Consider a camping vacation to avoid motel and food expenses. (Christian friends can pool the expenses of camping items.)

- Select vacation areas in your general locale.

- Use some family games in place of movies (like some of those unused games received at Christmas).

- To reduce expenses and increase fellowship, consider taking vacation trips with two or more families.

- If flying, use the least expensive coach fare. Flexibility in day of the week or even time of day can result in significant savings.

g. Clothing (5 percent of net income)

Many families in debt sacrifice this area in their budget because of excesses in other areas. Prudent planning and buying can clothe any family neatly without great expense.

- Save enough money to buy without using credit.

- Educate family members on care of clothing.

- Apply discipline with children to enforce these habits.

- Develop skills in making and mending clothing.

- Avoid the trap of fashion/fad consciousness—especially when it means buying expensive labels for no functional reason. When possible, buy clothes with a classic style that meet a need rather than clothes that make a temporary fashion statement.

Budget Hints

- Make a written list of clothing needs and purchase during the "off" season when possible.

- Select outfits that can be mixed and used in multiple combinations rather than as a single set.

- Shop the discount outlets that carry unmarked name-brand goods.

- Shop at authentic factory outlet stores for close-out values of top quality.

- Watch garage sales, consignment shops and Goodwill-type stores for outstanding values.

- Select clothing made of home-washable fabrics.

- Use coin-operated dry cleaning machines instead of commercial cleaners.

- Practice early repair for damaged clothing.

- Learn to utilize all clothing fully (especially children's wear).

h. Savings (5 percent of net income)

It is important to establish regular saving in your spending plan. Without a habit of saving, the use of credit and its resulting debt becomes a lifelong prison.

Savings Hints

- Use a company payroll withdrawal, if possible. This removes the money before you receive it.

- Use an automatic bank withdrawal from your checking account into your savings account.

- Write a check to your savings account just as if it were a creditor.

- Begin saving at least a small monthly amount now. When you have paid off all consumer debts, allocate those monthly amounts to savings.

i. Medical/dental expenses (6 percent of net income)

You must anticipate these expenses in your budget and set aside funds regularly; failure to do so will wreck your plans and lead to indebtedness. Do not sacrifice family health due to lack of planning; but, at the same time, do not use doctors excessively. Proper prevention is much cheaper than correction.

You can avoid many dental bills by teaching children to eat the right foods and to clean their teeth properly. Your dentist will supply all the information you need on this subject.

Many doctor bills can be avoided in the same way. Taking proper care of your body through diet, rest and exercise will usually reward you with good health. Abusing your body may not result in immediate consequences, but you will ultimately pay through illnesses and malfunctions. This is not to say that all illnesses or problems are caused by neglect, but a great many are.

Don't hesitate to question doctors and dentists in advance about costs. Also, educate yourself enough to discern when you are getting good value for your money. Most ethical professionals will not take offense at your questions. If they do, it may be a hint to change providers.

Shop around for prescriptions. You will be amazed at the wide variance in prices from one store to the next. Ask about generic drugs. These are usually much less expensive and are just as effective.

j. Miscellaneous and variable expenses (6 percent of net income)

Some of these expenses occur monthly, and others occur on an as-needed basis (such as appliances).

One of the most important factors in home expenses is you. If you can perform routine maintenance and repair, considerable expenses can be avoided. If, on the other hand, you are just handy enough to turn a $50 repair into a $200 mess, you'll need to decide whether you have the aptitude for a particular job. Still, routine maintenance is usually more of an "elbow grease" issue.

Many people rationalize not doing these things on the basis that their time is too valuable. Although this argument may have some merit for people who earn much more per hour than a repairman costs, unless they can earn it for as many hours as they want any time they want, it is probably a weak argument. And even for those who can earn around the clock, every hour of the day should not be tied up in the pursuit of money.

A part of care and maintenance around the home relates to family life, particularly the training of children. When they see Mom and Dad willing to do some physical labor to help around the home, they will learn good habits. But if you refuse to get involved, why should they? Where will they ever learn the skills of self-sufficiency?

Some men avoid working on home projects because they say they lack the necessary skills. Well, those skills are learned, not gifted. There are many good books, often found in your local library, that detail every area of home maintenance. At some point in the future, many of these skills are likely to be necessities rather than choices.

k. Investments (5 percent of net income)

Individuals and families with surplus income in their budgets will have the opportunity to invest for retirement or other long-term goals. This recommended percentage is a great starting amount, and then as debt-free status is achieved, more money can be diverted to this category.

l. School/Child care (5 percent of net income)

(If this category is used, other categories must be adjusted downward a total of 5 percent.)

A growing number of families choose private school and/or child care for their children. This category is for those expenses. Because this is an elective, it is not included within the normal 100 percent allotment, so other categories must be reduced to provide these funds.

m. Unallocated Surplus Income

Income from unallocated sources (garage sales, gifts) can be kept in the checking account and placed in this category. This category is also useful for recording income information for tax purposes.

Variable Income Planning

Families with variable monthly incomes need a spending plan even more than families on fixed salaries. Many people with fluctuating incomes get trapped into debt because they spend what they make during high-income months and borrow during lean months rather than anticipating and saving for them.

Living on a fluctuating income can be very deceiving—and difficult. Months of high income can easily be construed as the new norm or a windfall profit to be spent on non-necessities. To properly manage variable income, conservatively estimate what your annual income is likely to be. Divide it by 12, and then use that amount as the monthly income for your plan. Put all your income into a savings account and withdraw your plan amount each month.

This method will allow surplus funds from higher-income months to accumulate in the savings account to provide the normal planned income during months of actual lower income. This is not hoarding; it is planning according to Proverbs 6:6-8.

Pulling It All Together

Now that you have seen the general categories of expenses, one thing should be clear. Creating a spending plan is not mysterious magic. Nor is it too complicated. Although some people make a hobby of it and use sophisticated software that can generate a hundred different reports to give alternate views of the same information, others get by just fine with a fistful of hand-labeled envelopes.

The basic steps are simple.

1. Track all of your expenses for a month. Everything. (Include a monthly estimate for expenses you pay every three months or six months, etc.)

2. List your income for the month.

3. Compare the totals to determine whether you are spending more than you earn.

4. List your expenses in the category where they belong.

5. Check to see whether your category totals are within the suggested percentage of income.

6. Make any necessary adjustments (either to income or spending or both) to create a monthly surplus.

7. Spend according to plan, using discipline and patience to avoid violating your plan.

Remember that the race to accumulate usually ends at a different finish line than we expect. Effective advertising promises a finish line of wealth and happiness. Reality delivers a finish line of high stress, a crater of debt, and often the loss of the very things we worked so hard to get. Don't be the rabbit, getting caught up in the race.

Instead, be the tortoise, content to make slow, steady progress toward your goals. This is not hard; it's just countercultural. And it's God's way. *"The plans of the diligent lead to profit as surely as haste leads to poverty"* (Proverbs 21:5, NIV). The Contemporary English Version says it this way: *"If you plan and work hard, you will have plenty; if you get in a hurry, you will end up poor."*

Bottom line? You can do this. The forms at the end of the chapter will guide you. Go to CrownMoneyMap.org for additional help. A free online journey to developing financial faithfulness awaits you.

A Journey of Faith:
Glenn and Susan Preston

God, the Creator and Owner of all things, has promised to provide for our needs. We show our gratitude when we are accountable to Him through a budget that helps us spend wisely.

Glenn and Susan Preston of Oakwood, Georgia, can attest to the reality of that promise. They are the parents of six children ranging in ages from 2 to 16 years, but only Glenn works full time.

First exposure to Crown

Early in his life, Glenn was introduced to the teachings of Larry Burkett by a co-worker, Vicky Putman, and her husband Dennis.

"Dennis had listened to Larry's tapes in the mid-1980s and decided he wanted Vicky to stay home with the kids," Glenn says. "So he became his family's sole provider. He gave me a stack of Larry's tapes and explained the importance of living on a budget. He was living by those principles himself."

Unfortunately, Glenn wasn't completely ready to put Dennis' advice into practice. Not long after this, he married his wife Susan, and early in their marriage they had financial problems.

The couple moved to Auburn, Alabama, where he was going to attend graduate school and she planned to work full time. But six months after the wedding, Susan learned she was pregnant and chose to stay home with their child.

Glenn earned money through a teaching assistantship while attending graduate school to study physical education. He also worked from 3 p.m. to 11 p.m. on Saturdays and Sundays at a local hospital.

"It wasn't the smartest way to do things," he says. "I should have gotten a full-time job and gone to school part time."

However, God provided for the couple through a number of means, including help from their parents.

Crown for the second time

Glenn's physical education career eventually took him to North Georgia College and State University in Dahlonega, Georgia, where Don Delozier, an instructor for Crown, presented a seminar at his church.

Once again, Glenn was shown the need to handle his money according to God's financial principles.

He and Susan had a large amount of credit card debt, so he sought Don's help in developing a budget. "Don told us to be faithful and watch God bless," Glenn says, noting that he and Susan received an unexpected windfall that allowed them to completely repay their debts.

However, when Glenn moved into his current job as fitness center director and facilities coordinator at Gainesville College, he lost touch with his budget. He and Susan moved to Oakwood, Georgia, where the college is located, and their expenses changed. "I didn't update our budget," he says, "and our debt started mounting."

A third encounter with Crown

Recently, Glenn went through Crown's life group study, which takes participants through a deep journey into God's Word.

"I had done the mechanical part," he says, "but the Scriptures made the difference. This time I got a heart transplant. I had never seen that the way you handle money affects your intimacy with Christ. Every day you're in the study, you're in the Scriptures, and the Scriptures will change your heart."

One portion of the study that impressed Susan was the chapter on work. She has since started a small home business selling gourmet foods, which gives her an occasional break and fellowship with other women. Susan is also teaching biblical financial principles to middle school girls at her church.

In late January, Glenn and Susan had the opportunity to tell people across the nation about the manner in which God has changed their finances. During a CBS television special about the growing national interest in the Bible's view on money, Crown Financial Ministries was featured. A CBS camera crew set up their equipment in the couple's home and allowed them to share their story.

"For Susan and me, Crown has been life-changing," Glenn says. "We appreciate the time and effort put into the resources Crown provides.

Action Steps

_____

_____

_____

_____

_____

Celebration Plan

_____

_____

_____

_____

_____

Estimated Spending Plan

Date _____   **SAMPLE**

MONTHLY INCOME

GROSS MONTHLY INCOME — **$3,790**
- Salary — 3,750
- Interest — 5
- Dividends — 15
- Other Income — 20

Less

1. **Tithe/Giving** — 379
2. **Taxes** (Federal, State, FICA) — 750

NET SPENDABLE INCOME — **$2,661**

MONTHLY LIVING EXPENSES

3. **Housing** — **$853**
   - Mortgage/Rent — 650
   - Insurance — 20
   - Property taxes — 50
   - Cable TV — 0
   - Electricity — 60
   - Gas — 12
   - Water — 10
   - Sanitation — 0
   - Telephone — 25
   - Maintenance — 26
   - Internet service — 0
   - Other — 0

4. **Food** — 373

5. **Transportation** — 345
   - Payments — 100
   - Gas & Oil — 75
   - Insurance — 50
   - License/Taxes — 40
   - Maintenance — 50
   - Replacement — 30
   - Other — 0

6. **Insurance** — 105
   - Life — 40
   - Health/Dental — 65
   - Disability — 0

- Other — 0

7. **Debts** (not including house or auto) — 133

8. **Entertainment/Recreation** — 133
   - Eating out — 83
   - Babysitters — 0
   - Activities/Trips — 20
   - Vacation — 30
   - Pets — 0
   - Other — 0

9. **Clothing** — 133

10. **Savings** — 133

11. **Medical/Dental** — 160
    - Doctor — 60
    - Dentist — 50
    - Prescriptions — 50
    - Other — 0

12. **Miscellaneous** — 160
    - Toiletries/Cosmetics — 19
    - Beauty/Barber — 20
    - Laundry/Cleaners — 15
    - Allowances — 45
    - Subscriptions — 15
    - Gifts — 46
    - Other — 0

13. **Investments** — 133

14. **School/Child Care** — 0
    - Tuition — 0
    - Materials — 0
    - Transportation — 0
    - Day care — 0

TOTAL LIVING EXPENSES — **$2,661**

HOW THE MONTH TURNS OUT

NET SPENDABLE INCOME — **$2,661**

- TOTAL LIVING EXPENSES — **$2,661**

= SURPLUS OR DEFICIT — 0

Estimated Spending Plan

Date _____

MONTHLY INCOME

GROSS MONTHLY INCOME _____

    Salary _____
    Interest _____
    Dividends _____
    Other Income _____

Less

1. **Tithe/Giving** _____
2. **Taxes** (Federal, State, FICA) _____

NET SPENDABLE INCOME _____

MONTHLY LIVING EXPENSES

3. **Housing** _____
    Mortgage/Rent _____
    Insurance _____
    Property taxes _____
    Cable TV _____
    Electricity _____
    Gas _____
    Water _____
    Sanitation _____
    Telephone _____
    Maintenance _____
    Internet service _____
    Other _____

4. **Food** _____

5. **Transportation** _____
    Payments _____
    Gas & Oil _____
    Insurance _____
    License/Taxes _____
    Maintenance _____
    Replacement _____
    Other _____

6. **Insurance** _____
    Life _____
    Health/Dental _____
    Disability _____

    Other _____

7. **Debts** (not including house or auto) _____

8. **Entertainment/Recreation** _____
    Eating out _____
    Babysitters _____
    Activities/Trips _____
    Vacation _____
    Pets _____
    Other _____

9. **Clothing** _____

10. **Savings** _____

11. **Medical/Dental** _____
    Doctor _____
    Dentist _____
    Prescriptions _____
    Other _____

12. **Miscellaneous** _____
    Toiletries/Cosmetics _____
    Beauty/Barber _____
    Laundry/Cleaners _____
    Allowances _____
    Subscriptions _____
    Gifts _____
    Other _____

13. **Investments** _____

14. **School/Child Care** _____
    Tuition _____
    Materials _____
    Transportation _____
    Day care _____

TOTAL LIVING EXPENSES _____

HOW THE MONTH TURNS OUT

NET SPENDABLE INCOME _____

- TOTAL LIVING EXPENSES _____

= SURPLUS OR DEFICIT _____

Percentage Spending Plan

Date _____   **SAMPLE**

Annual Income: $ 45,480					
Gross Income				$	3,790
1. Tithe/Giving				$	379
2. Taxes				$	750
Net Spendable Income				$	2,661

Spending Category	Percentage		NSI*		Amount
3. Housing	32%	X	2,661	= $	853
4. Food	13%	X	2,661	= $	345
5. Transportation	13%	X	2,661	= $	345
6. Insurance	5%	X	2,661	= $	133
7. Debts	5%	X	2,661	= $	133
8. Entertainment/Recreation	5%	X	2,661	= $	133
9. Clothing	5%	X	2,661	= $	133
10. Savings	5%	X	2,661	= $	133
11. Medical/Dental	6%	X	2,661	= $	160
12. Miscellaneous	6%	X	2,661	= $	160
13. Investments	5%	X	2,661	= $	133
14. School/Child Care[1]	0%	X	0	= $	0
Total (cannot exceed Net Spendable Income)				$	2,661

*Net Spendable Income
[1] If you have this expense, this percentage must be deducted from other spending plan categories.

Percentage Spending Plan

Date _____

Annual Income: $_____			
Gross Income			$_____
1. Tithe/Giving			$_____
2. Taxes			$_____
Net Spendable Income			$_____

Spending Category	Percentage		NSI*		Amount
3. Housing	_____	X	_____	=	$_____
4. Food	_____	X	_____	=	$_____
5. Transportation	_____	X	_____	=	$_____
6. Insurance	_____	X	_____	=	$_____
7. Debts	_____	X	_____	=	$_____
8. Entertainment/Recreation	_____	X	_____	=	$_____
9. Clothing	_____	X	_____	=	$_____
10. Savings	_____	X	_____	=	$_____
11. Medical/Dental	_____	X	_____	=	$_____
12. Miscellaneous	_____	X	_____	=	$_____
13. Investments	_____	X	_____	=	$_____
14. School/Child Care [1]	_____	X	_____	=	$_____
Total (cannot exceed Net Spendable Income)					$_____

*Net Spendable Income
[1] If you have this expense, this percentage must be deducted from other spending plan categories.

MAJOR PURCHASES

Buying Houses and Cars

Major purchases are inevitable. Most people expect to buy a house or a car at some point. Even a new refrigerator at $1,000 to $2,000 can be a challenge.

Although it is possible for any expense category to get out of line and ruin a spending plan, nothing will do it quicker than a major purchase. But it doesn't have to be that way.

Think of major purchases as wild mustangs invading your fenced corral. They threaten to scatter your horses, leaving you with nothing. You could build a higher, stronger fence and keep them out, but you would rather have the benefits they offer. What if you could tame them enough to allow them into the corral and keep them there?

This is what we are about to do. Careful planning can tame the major purchases that threaten to destroy our finances by causing us to spend more than we earn. With wise planning and applying biblical wisdom, you can successfully make major purchases and develop a lifestyle of financial faithfulness at the same time.

Housing

Let's talk first about the cost of housing. Since it is the greatest expense most of us ever incur, we should carefully consider several complex variables before making a commitment. And because we are in management of God's possessions, our first responsibility is to pray for His guidance regarding all financial decisions.

Carefully research the housing market along with available financing. Your personal situation—including your spending plan, which is detailed in Chapter 1—also sheds light on whether buying or renting is best at any given time.

Your spending plan lets you know how much is coming in, how much is going out, and areas in which you can cut costs. This allows you to take the monthly amount you would be required to pay on a certain house and see whether it will fit.

Buying a house without first making sure it fits your spending plan can place a tremendous financial burden on your family. Limiting yourself to a house within your spending plan may require you to settle for a smaller house than you desire, but one thing is for sure: The less you owe on your house, the sooner you can pay it off.

Then, you can take the money you were using to make payments and invest it for your children's college or for retirement. The state of our nation's economy is another reason to pay off your house early. The continuous buildup of federal debt must eventually produce severe economic consequences—especially for individuals with heavy debt burdens.

Having a written spending plan and living within it is the first step in buying a house. Although your financial situation will be the major factor in determining what type of housing you need, there are other factors to consider. Prayerfully give these questions some thought.

1. Is your job secure enough for you to make mortgage payments? If not, consider renting instead of buying.

2. How long do you plan to stay in the area? If you know you will be staying in the community for at least five years, house ownership may be a good option.

3. What is the economy like in the area you are considering? Is the area growing substantially? Will the house appreciate? You don't want to be stuck with a house that is hard to sell because of the local economy.

4. What is the cost of living in the new area? If it is high, it will definitely affect your budget and may change the amount you can afford for housing.

After answering these questions, take the amount you can spend for housing and determine if house payments, including taxes, insurance, maintenance, and utilities would be equal to or less than rental payments for a similar house in the same area. If they are, then buying a house may be a wise choice.

Biblical Principles Regarding Debt

Since we've already covered this subject in the Debt and Bankruptcy chapter, we'll limit this discussion to a few reminders.

1. The Bible doesn't prohibit borrowing, but it does discourage it. In fact, every biblical reference to borrowing is a negative one.

2. Borrowing is literally a vow to repay, and God requires us to keep our vows.

3. Surety means taking on an obligation to pay without a guaranteed way to pay it.

Until the 1980s, many banks did not require a personal guarantee (surety) for a home loan. They allowed the home to stand as sole collateral. In today's economy, however, with higher costs and lower down payments, the rules have changed.

Since most homeowners can no longer avoid surety, we recommend that you:

1. buy a home well within your means,

2. make a large enough down payment to reduce the potential risk,

3. and pay off the mortgage as quickly as possible.

With wisdom-filled planning, your home purchase can be more fun, exciting, and peaceful than you ever imagined!

Housing Options

If you've decided that buying a house fits into your spending plan and is in your best long-term interest, you can begin to look at the options available to you. Included in these options are new and used houses, condominiums, and mobile homes.

New House Pros ☺ and Cons ☹

☺ You can design it to fit your individual needs.

☹ It will probably cost much more than you think after paying for changes and upgrades, hidden expenses, window treatments, landscaping, etc.

☹ Overseeing the construction of a new house requires many decisions and takes considerable time and effort.

Used House Pros ☺ and Cons ☹

☺ You know exactly what the house will cost.

☺ It will likely come with many extras included: curtains, curtain rods, towel racks, ceiling fans, lights in the closets, light bulbs, an established lawn, shrubbery, and occasionally even appliances. Be sure the contract states exactly which items will come with the house.

☹ The condition may show wear and tear, which means repairs. The older the house is, the more repairs it's likely to need. Always check the heating and air conditioning, roof, water heater, and appliances to see if they are in working condition. You may choose to hire a house inspection service to do this for you. (Ask your Real Estate agent for a recommendation). After the house has been checked, you can decide whether to purchase the house as is or back out of the deal.

The Fixer-Upper or Handyman's Special

Fixer-uppers usually sell for well below normal market price. Some of this is due to their lack of visual appeal. If you can look past this, you may have a diamond in the rough. Keep in mind, though, that some of the lower price will be lost through above-average repair costs.

Be sure to have the house checked thoroughly, including foundations, roof, plumbing, and wiring, so you know exactly what is wrong with the house before you buy it. If you have the skills and don't mind doing the repairs, you can make a nice profit when you sell it.

Condominiums

Make sure you know all additional costs, such as maintenance fees and club fees, and have them factored into your spending plan.

Be aware that the maintenance fees are subject to change each year, and you have no control over them. This is not a bad option, especially if you don't want to bother with yard work.

Mobile Homes

Although some people won't consider living in manufactured housing, others think they are a great value.

As with a car, a new mobile home may lose about 25 percent of its total value when it leaves the sales lot. Consider buying a previously owned mobile home, because someone else has already taken the depreciation.

Financing

Now that you've decided what type of house you want to buy, you need to decide how to pay for it.

Pay Cash

The best way to buy a house is to pay cash. Our modern culture wants too much too fast, making this approach the rare exception. A good compromise, however, is to

- buy a smaller house,

- invest time and effort into improving its value,

- sell it, and

- buy the next larger size house.

This approach rewards the patient with their dream house and little or no debt.

Institutional Loans

These loans, issued by banks, savings and loans, credit unions, and mortgage companies, are the most common type of financing for a house purchase. It's important to shop around, because there are so many variables in the rates and terms.

Fees and Contracts

Most institutional loans require a down payment, usually between 5 and 20 percent. But remember, the more you put down, the less likely you are to have a problem with surety.

In addition, there are various closing costs.

- Loan origination fees
- Points
- Attorneys' fees
- Survey fees
- Inspection fees
- Appraisal fees
- PMI (private mortgage insurance)
- Real estate commissions
- Credit reports
- Title search fees

These fees can add up to quite an expense—several thousand dollars—and should be researched thoroughly when considering any loan. Many times the seller may pay for some or all of the closing costs.

If your offer to purchase the house is subject to selling your present house, getting financial approval, or waiting on results from various inspections, be sure these contingencies are included in the contract.

You would be wise to have the property tested for any conditions that might apply, including radon gas, termites, structural defects, water problems, and non-working appliances.

Fixed-rate Mortgages

The fixed-rate mortgage is an excellent house loan. You know exactly what the interest rate and monthly mortgage payment will be and whether it will fit into your budget.

Although a fixed-rate loan will have a slightly higher interest rate than adjustable-rate loans, it is well worth the additional cost if you anticipate keeping the loan for several years. You have the benefit of knowing that your monthly principal and interest payment will not change during the life of the loan.

The shorter the mortgage, the less interest you will pay. A 15-year mortgage usually has three advantages over a 30-year:

1. You cut your risk in half by owning your home free and clear in half the time.

2. You pay much less interest because of the shorter time.

3. You can usually get a better interest rate (by a half-percent) for a 15-year.

Nevertheless, many people are better off to get a 30-year mortgage and treat it as a 15-year. By making larger payments than the required minimum, they can reduce the term to 15 years or even less, achieving the first two advantages shown above. But if they encounter a difficult financial stretch, they are not required to make a payment as large as the 15-year mortgage would demand.

Since rates vary from institution to institution and from week to week, shop around for the best rates and terms.

Adjustable Rate Mortgages (ARMs)

ARMs are not a bad option under certain conditions. If you can answer "yes" to these three questions, an ARM might be attractive for your situation.

1. Do you plan to sell the house or refinance the loan within two to three years?

2. Will your initial rate be at least 1 to 2 percent lower than the

fixed rate?

3. Does the loan put caps on the maximum annual interest-rate increase as well as the absolute maximum during the life of the loan?

Since these loans fluctuate with the economy, it's crucial to know exactly how high the interest rate could go.

Most ARMs begin with an interest rate that's a percentage point or two below current fixed-rate loans; then they periodically adjust after that. This allows more people to qualify for them, but it also makes it harder to determine how much to allocate for housing from year to year in your spending plan.

Be sure you understand the terms before you choose an ARM. For example, if you get a 7 percent ARM with a 5 percent cap, your rate could climb to 12 percent. Let's suppose the current fixed rate is 9 percent. If the terms of the adjustable are such that you could go above the fixed rate of 9 percent after just two or three years, then you probably are better off taking the fixed rate.

You also need to consider whether your budget can make the payments if the ARM goes up to the maximum.

Payday or Bi-monthly Mortgages

These mortgages are designed to increase the frequency of your loan payments. Instead of paying a monthly payment, you pay one-half the monthly payment every other week or one-quarter of the payment every week. This type of mortgage payment results in one extra payment per year.

Since part of the payment is applied to the principal earlier and an extra payment is made each year, equity accrues at a faster rate. You pay off the loan sooner and save interest. Most lenders who offer this option make an additional charge for it, partially offsetting the advantage. You can avoid these charges completely by staying with an ordinary mortgage and simply paying a little more than required every month.

Assumable Mortgages

These mortgages rarely exist anymore. If you find a house for sale with an assumable mortgage, the remaining amount of the mortgage will probably be low because it doesn't have many years left. Check the terms carefully before placing a lot of value on it.

Government Financing

VA, FHA, and state-bonded programs may be obtained through your local banking institution. They may have lower interest rates and lower down payments.

Seller Financing (Land Sale Contract, Trust Deed)

Some sellers will finance a house for the buyer. This provides a steady income to the seller, and the buyer usually saves on closing costs. Be sure a qualified attorney draws up all the legal papers so there is no question about the terms of the sale.

Equity Sharing

Equity sharing is an excellent way for a buyer to get help in purchasing a house. It also allows an investor to receive a healthy return on a relatively small investment. Here is how it works.

1. A buyer who needs help raising a down payment finds an investor willing to loan part of it.

2. They write an agreement that specifies a period of years that the buyer must live in the house before selling it and the amount of equity the investors receive upon sale. Although they can agree on any terms they choose, it is common for the investors to receive their initial investment back plus 50 percent of any profit.

It's possible that when the agreed-upon selling time comes, the original buyer will want to continue living there. This situation should be dealt with in advance—when the agreement is written—by including a provision that says the investor's loan will be repaid with a predetermined amount of interest. To avoid misunderstandings and strained relationships, a good Christian attorney should be involved in the preparation of any equity-sharing plan.

Parent-Assisted Financing

Many parents delight in helping their children reasonably—being careful to not take all the burdens off them. Consider this scenario. Parents provide the down payment for a son or daughter to buy a house. The house is in joint ownership: the parents own part and the children own part. The parents make the payments on the house and then rent it to the children for an amount equal to the payments. The parents depreciate the house, taking the deduction off their taxes. The children are responsible for repairing and maintaining the house, and when they eventually sell it, they receive the profit.

This method of financing benefits both parents and children. It may also be used by Christians who are willing to help other young Christian couples get their first house.

Parents with substantial savings may also choose to be lenders for their children—making the mortgage themselves. This saves money on closing costs and can provide a source of retirement income for the parents. They will need to gauge their children's maturity and make sure they are responsible enough to handle this generosity without either being spoiled or taking advantage of their parents.

Parental financing should be viewed by both parties with the same financial commitment and consequences as any other type of financing.

All legal forms should be on record so there will be no questions if the parents or the children pass away or if there is a default.

Refinance Issues

If interest rates fall after you buy your house, you'll probably be tempted to refinance. But just because rates are 1 or 2 percent lower doesn't mean you should refinance immediately.

First, determine the dollar amount of interest you would save through refinancing and compare that to the costs of new loan fees, title searches, surveys, and appraisals.

If you can easily reclaim these expenses through the savings in interest within a few years, refinancing is a good idea for you. You'll usually benefit from refinancing if the new rate is at least 3 percent lower than the rate on your present mortgage.

Whatever financing option you choose, pray earnestly for God's wisdom and give Him an opportunity to show you the best option. Trust Him to reveal each step in the process, and have an attitude of expectancy.

Questions and Answers

What Happens If the Bank Forecloses on My House?

Although foreclosure is a serious problem, it does not mean God has washed His hands of you. As a result of losing a house, you will learn a costly but valuable lesson on the danger of surety.

When you enter into a contract, you are bound by your word to fulfill its intent. As Psalm 37:21 says, *"The wicked borrows and does not pay back, but the righteous is gracious and gives."*

Once the foreclosure has been finalized, work out a payment plan for the difference between the amount of your mortgage and the price the lender receives from the sale of the house. Be sure this payment plan will fit into your adjusted budget.

The lender will always have the option to file a deficiency judgment against you and may retain this right for several years. Check your state laws. The lender may choose to release you from the deficiency debt and has the right to do so. You must commit to pay the deficiency and do whatever the lender requests.

If you are fortunate enough to deed the house as total payment to the lender instead of going through foreclosure, you may avoid paying anything, but you will still lose the house and equity.

If you've fallen behind on your payment or must move quickly, make every effort to sell your house, even if you have to take a loss. Since foreclosed houses are generally sold at auction for much less than fair market value, the ease of letting someone else handle it will probably cost you a bundle.

What Type of Insurance Should I Have on My House?

Most lending institutions require that you have enough insurance to cover the amount of the mortgage. A homeowner's policy is a comprehensive insurance plan that covers the house, its contents, and any liability associated with the property. It is the best and least expensive way to insure a dwelling.

Costs vary significantly from one insurance company to another, so shop carefully before you buy any kind of insurance. Most insurance companies provide special insurance for condominiums and mobile homes as well.

Should I Have Life Insurance on My House?

Yes. Commonly called mortgage life insurance, it's usually sold through the lender from whom you received your house loan. But this can be a very expensive way to purchase life insurance. A decreasing term insurance policy through your local insurance agent may be less expensive.

The best approach is to determine what your total life insurance needs are and include your house loan balance with this.

By purchasing one policy, you will save money, compared to the cost of several life insurance policies. As your need for death protection diminishes, you can reduce your coverage.

Your House as an Investment

Historically, the best overall investment for most Americans has been

EFFECTS OF PAYING MORE EACH MONTH ON A $100,000 MORTGAGE AT 9 PERCENT				
Extra amount paid	Principal/ Interest	Life of loan (years)	Interest paid	Interest saved
None	$804.62	30.00	$189,667.95	0
$25 monthly	$829.62	26.17	$160,222.62	$29,445.33
$50 monthly	$854.62	23.42	$140,227.01	$49,440.94
$100 monthly	**$904.62**	**19.75**	**$113,872.30**	**$75,795.65**

their houses, which have kept track with inflation and appreciated an average of approximately four percent a year. Generalities and averages, however, do not apply to every situation, and past performance never offers a guarantee for future performance.

One geographical region (even a micro-region within a city) may increase dramatically in price while its neighbor remains flat. The following year could see the flat neighbor appreciate while the first region actually depreciates.

Consequently, your personal residence should not be viewed primarily as an investment, although it offers the likely benefit of appreciation over time as well as a place to live.

In spite of market fluctuations, the desirability of personal home ownership is not likely to change unless we experience another Great Depression, in which case all other investments are equally at risk. If you can't pay your real estate taxes in a bad economy, you can lose your house in three years (in most states). However, if you can't pay the mortgage payments, you can lose it in three months.

It is unfortunate that most Americans have come to accept long-term debt on their houses as normal. The high expense of housing—particularly in some markets—requires most young couples to get a 30-year mortgage to make the monthly payments affordable. However, by controlling their lifestyle and prepaying their principal a little bit each month, most families can pay off a house in 15 years or so.

A simple investment strategy to follow is to make the ownership of your house your first investment priority. Then use the monthly mortgage payments you were making to start your savings for education or retirement.

Financial institutions are in the business of loaning money, and they have done a good job of inducing us to borrow. More than 70 percent of Americans under age 65 do not own their houses debt free.

There is no better time to start paying off your debts than right now, and it begins with an attitude adjustment. This adjustment is to make up your mind that God's Word—not someone else's idea of financial logic—governs your decisions.

Cars

Owning a car is the norm in our society. Outside of the largest urban areas where public transportation is sufficient, owning at least one car is a practical necessity. So what is the most economical way to buy one?

Examine Your Motives

Most cars are sold because of buyers' wants rather than their needs. In fact, most car shoppers are simply tired of their current car; it looks out of date or needs some repairs. In many cases, they want to keep up with their neighbors or coworkers. Sometimes they just need a mood adjustment, which a new car certainly provides—for a short time.

We have been programmed to think that if any of these conditions exist we need a new car. Certainly cars do wear out, and we will all eventually need to get another car; but we should examine our motives first to make sure we are not caving in to an emotional need rather than a transportation need. A different car can solve a transportation need, but it will only deepen the emotional need if it involves a greater debt burden.

Bottom line—buy an automobile for the right reason, and pray for His wisdom when you begin the buying process.

Determine Your Needs

Having examined your motives, the next step is to determine your needs. Who wouldn't like to drive the latest greatest? Unfortunately, may people shop with this perspective: "I'll find the car I want, and if the salesman can come up with financing that allows me to drive it off, it must be God's will." That's a disaster in the making.

Consider these questions:

1. What do I need?

2. What is the best value?

3. What does my spending plan allow (considering all ownership costs)?

4. What is the best stewardship of my family's hard-earned money?

Costs (payments, insurance, maintenance) for a mid-range new car commonly run in excess of $500 a month. That kind of expense can wreck the average family's spending plan.

Sure, they may be able to make the monthly payments, but the other categories, like Food and Clothes, will begin to suffer. Since these are major needs, the family will inevitably go into debt to get them.

The average family needs to buy a good quality, reliable used car. The size, style, age, and appearance of that car will vary from family to family. Unfortunately, many people can't overcome the temptation to buy a new car. Furthermore, a young couple who buys a new car may be starting a lifetime habit. They may become accustomed to buying every four years, which can cost an incredible amount of money, especially if these new car purchases are made on credit.

Dr. Floyd Vest, with the mathematics department at the University of North Texas, has calculated the financial impact of a family buying a new car on credit every four years beginning in 1990. The illustration family always has two cars, one of which is four years older than the other. When the older one is eight years old, they trade it for a new one.

Using constant factors for each purchase (5 percent inflation, 12 percent interest, 20 percent down payment), it proves the tremendous expense of regular new car purchases. The illustration family paid $15,000 for the first new car. Beginning with the third car, the 20 percent down payment was assumed to come entirely from the trade-in value of the eight-year-old car being replaced.

Over a 56-year period, the family spent more than $1.25 million on new cars! This is much more than the average home purchase expense. And imagine the investment that would accumulate if some of this money were put to work for you rather than against you.

Be an Informed Buyer

Doing your homework before you begin shopping for a car can help you find the car best suited to your needs.

Consumer advocacy groups and publications, such as *Consumer Reports*, track the safety, maintenance, and value of each model. And remember that cheaper does not always mean better.

Friends and family members are also a good source of information. Talk with owners of cars similar to the model you are considering to see if they are satisfied.

The Old Gas Mileage Excuse

It's very common for couples to justify buying a new car because it gets better gas mileage than their existing car. Usually, they're just tired of their existing car and need an excuse to buy a new one.

Crown has coached many people who bought new cars on the basis of mileage. Unfortunately, until they sat down with a counselor, they never figured out just how much mileage savings it would take to equal the cost of a new car. In some cases, they would have to drive their new car almost 50 years to reap mileage savings equal to the car's cost.

Shopping For a Used Car

Once you have determined the type of car you want and can afford, the next step is to find it. Go to your closest friends first. Let them know you're looking for a car. Find out if there is a family in your church with a car to sell that will fit your need.

Before most Christians will sell their cars to people they know, they will either reveal everything that is wrong with the cars or else have them fixed.

By purchasing directly from the owner, you can learn the history of the car and usually negotiate the best possible price.

Leasing Companies

A second good source of used cars is a leasing company. Many of these companies keep their cars one or two years and then resell them.

Most of these cars have been routinely maintained, have low mileage, and are sold for a fair price. Often a car obtained from a leasing company will have a one-year warranty.

Banks

Bankers are another good source of used cars. Let your banker know you are interested in a really good repossession if one comes in.

Be aware that a repossessed car may need some repairs, since its owner most likely couldn't afford to maintain it properly. Have money in reserve for this purpose.

Car Dealers

Dealers have the largest selection of used cars available. A used car that was locally owned can be a good deal if you're able to contact the previous owner to see if the car has any hidden problems.

Advertisements

The difficulty in using this source for used cars is that you don't know the seller, and the seller doesn't know you. Unfortunately, there are a lot of unethical people with cars for sale.

Before buying any used car, it is advisable to write an affidavit saying, "I swear that the car I am selling, to my knowledge, has no obvious defects, no rust that I know about, and no false odometer reading." Have the seller sign it (before a notary if possible). Most honest people won't object, and most dishonest ones won't sign it.

Finally, have a mechanic check the car for defects or problems that may not be obvious to you, such as hidden rust, signs of having been in an accident, and engine problems. The dollars you spend having a mechanic look at the car are peanuts compared to the grief and expense you could be forced to deal with later.

Used Car Buying Tips

Before buying a used car, first determine what kind of car you want. Otherwise, you could be led in many different directions.

Perhaps the make and model you want is available as a "program car." These are lease and rental cars that have been bought back by dealers. They offer low mileage and a lower price than you'd pay for the same make and model if you bought it new.

When buying a used car, check a number of key areas for problems. Open all doors, the trunk, and the hood to see if the car has been repainted.

It may be that the vehicle was involved in a front- or rear-end collision. If you look under the hood and find the stickers are missing, that's a good sign that the car has been repainted.

When checking the engine, open the oil cap. If it's black inside and you see burnt oil on the valves, you know there's a problem. You also can pull out the dipstick to check for water in the oil. In addition, you can rev up the engine to check for valve or lifter noise or rod knocking.

Of course, steam coming out from under the hood and smoke coming out from the exhaust are signs of problems.

Brakes are another item you want to check. If the car shakes or vibrates when you brake, it may be an indication that a rotor is warped. Also check the brake pads. When the pads wear completely down, the metal portion of the brake scrapes against the rotor or drum and causes serious damage.

Also check:

- Air conditioning
- Tires for remaining tread
- Lights and electrical system (be sure everything works, including the radio, automatic seat belts, adjustable seats, windows, all other electronic components)
- Upholstery
- Carpet

It is best to have the car checked by a reliable mechanic.

Finally, before you visit any dealership, research your market area and find an established dealer who ranks high in customer satisfaction.

Safety Considerations

According to the Insurance Institute for Highway Safety in Arlington, Virginia, safety has become a major consideration—right along with quality—for people buying a car.

You obviously want to protect yourself and your family to the greatest extent possible. But there's a secondary reason for this concern about safety, and that reason is financial.

Consider this scenario: You're driving in the rain and you stop suddenly to avoid hitting a dog in the road. Because your vehicle is not equipped with antilock brakes, the brakes lock up and your car slides off the road. The land beside the road is relatively flat and clear, allowing the car to slow down before it finally comes to rest against a tree.

No one is hurt, but the side of the car is damaged and will need expensive repairs. If your car had been equipped with antilock brakes, you might have avoided the accident. More importantly, antilock brakes could help you avoid a more serious accident in which someone could be seriously hurt.

One other general safety consideration: Small cars are not as safe as larger ones. In relation to their numbers on the road, small cars account for about twice as many deaths as large cars.

Buying the Car

A listener to one of our radio programs once wrote,

"We're considering buying a new car. But with new car prices so high, we can't afford the payments on a three-year note. Our bank offers a six-year loan with a balloon payment after three years. My husband likes this plan because he says we'll obviously be making a lot higher salary by then. But the whole concept of this frightens me. What do you think?"

Buying cars with long-term loans is like playing economic roulette. Consider several problems with this six-year balloon note.

1. This woman's husband was presuming on the future. He was presuming that he and his wife would be making higher salaries when this balloon note comes due in three years.

2. He wanted a car that was too expensive for his family's spending plan. If he and his wife couldn't afford to save money and pay cash for the car, they shouldn't buy a car that expensive.

3. He wanted a car that he couldn't pay off before it was totally depreciated, which is another indication that the car was too expensive for his family's spending plan.

4. He wasn't in agreement with his wife about buying the car. God works through both the husband and the wife in a marriage. They are a team. Genesis 2:24 says the husband and wife are one person. A divided mind on a financial issue is a red flag.

Get the most out of your existing car, and while you're driving it, set

aside money for your next one. In most cases, it is a lot less expensive to repair your car than to replace it. When it makes more economic sense to replace it, consider a good used car.

Proverbs 10:22 says the blessing of the Lord should be the thing that makes us rich, not worldly possessions. God's blessing will add no sorrow to our lives, but when we buy things that exceed our spending plan, we lose our peace of mind. Long-term loans for a car we can't afford will add a lot of sorrow to our lives.

The best way to finance a car is not to finance it at all! It is always the best policy to save the money and pay cash for your car. Auto financing is poor stewardship. If, in spite of this counsel, you find that you must finance a car, here are some good basic guidelines.

Do Not Finance Through the Car Dealership

Arrange a loan through a bank or other financial institution ahead of time so you can negotiate with the dealer on a cash basis. Be sure it is a simple interest loan with no pay-off restrictions. If you do that, at least you have the capability to become debt free in a short period of time.

Do Not Trade in Your Old Car; Sell It Instead

If a car dealer can sell your car and make a profit, so can you. It takes more time and effort to sell your car, but the effort is worthwhile. Advertise in the newspaper and online and put a sign in the car window. If your car is in reasonable shape, it shouldn't take very long to sell.

The main goal when purchasing an automobile is to educate yourself, pray for wisdom, expect God to meet your needs, and enjoy the experience of knowing that God wants His best for you.

Frequently Asked Questions And Answers

Should I Buy an Extended Warranty on My New Car?

If you are considering an extended warranty, ask questions.

1. Does the warranty cover a period of time or a number of miles not covered under any implied warranties?
2. Does the extended warranty cover parts and labor, or parts only?
3. Does the price of the warranty seem reasonable in relation to the price of the parts covered?

If an extended warranty covers 5 years/50,000 miles, then the coverage will probably last less than five years because the average person drives more than 10,000 miles per year. A better warranty would cover 5 years/100,000 miles.

If only parts are covered, the cost of labor is usually so great that the owner won't get the full benefit of buying the extended warranty unless each part covered is more expensive than the relative cost of the warranty.

How Much of Our Family Budget Should Be Designated for Car Expenses?

About 13 percent of your Net Spendable Income (income after deducting tithe and taxes) should be allotted for car expenses. These expenses include payments, gas, oil, maintenance, insurance, and some savings for a future replacement of the vehicle.

What Are Some Ways I Can Cut My Car Expenses?

1. Look for savings on car insurance. If your car is more than five years old, you may want to consider only liability coverage, which is required by law. Or you might choose a policy with a higher deductible. Shop and compare prices.

2. Save money on tires. Go to a tire dealer and ask if he sells "take-offs," which are tires that have been taken off a new car because the buyer wanted a different kind. Take-offs are nearly new and may be half the price.

3. Consider starting a car maintenance co-op or join an existing one. A typical co-op involves a group of Christians who meet regularly at a church parking lot to perform routine maintenance and car repairs for one another.

Preventive maintenance will save on towing charges due to unexpected breakdowns on the highway. Check your local library for books on car ownership that offer other money-saving tips.

What About Leasing a Car?

Leasing seems attractive to those who cannot otherwise afford a new car. But as the old saying goes, there is no free lunch.

The average new car is over $20,000, and as soon as you drive it off the lot you have a used car with a new car loan on it.

Loans involve down payments, and some people don't have enough savings to meet even this requirement. Since leasing involves little or no down payment, it is a convenient way to get a new car. But that convenience comes at a high price because there is more involved than just monthly payments.

It definitely costs more to lease a car than to purchase one over the same period of time because of the higher processing expense of a complex lease agreement and the added profit layer of the lease itself. Although leasing companies have the advantage of buying cars at a volume discount, the discount isn't much greater than an astute buyer can get on his own.

At the end of a lease period, you still owe a percentage of the car's value if you want to buy it. So you don't avoid the costs. You just string them out over a longer period of time. And then there are the potential penalties at the end of the lease:

1. If you drive too many miles (usually more than 10,000 per year), you'll pay a steep penalty for each excess mile.

2. If the car has "excessive" wear, you could pay another 10 percent. And if the car is generally downgraded, you could be required to pay an additional 10 percent.

You can watch the mileage during the lease term to gauge your excess mileage penalties, but the other potential penalties are more subjective, leaving you in jeopardy until you return the car.

In general, leasing is a better value when the costs can be deducted as a business expense, but most families cannot do this.

Bouncing Back:
Charlie and Julia Sizemore

Although saving for future purchases was once a way of life, it has become a lost art in today's credit culture. Charlie and Julia Sizemore, whose family is well on its way to getting out of debt after years of relying on credit cards, have rediscovered its value.

"I've got an engineering degree and a master's in business," Charlie said. "For years I've been in control of and responsible for multimillion-dollar operations, and I could do it well. I could nail a million-dollar budget within 2 percent, but I could not get within 15 percent of a home budget."

Charlie's 20-plus-year career as a petroleum engineer has been a rocky road for him, his wife Julia, and their two teenage daughters, Lindsay and Kristen.

He entered Texas Tech University during the Texas oil boom of the 1970s, when significant financial benefits were assured to recent petroleum engineering grads.

Three years later, right before he graduated, the oil boom had become an oil bust, and Charlie's career since has been marked by multiple layoffs, withdrawals from the Texas Employment Commission, long-distance commuting, and relocating.

Julia nodded with a smile. "The wives have a joke. It's not 'Has your husband been laid off?' but 'How many times has your husband been laid off?'"

Like many of his coworkers, Charlie and his family weathered the bad times by depending on credit cards.

"When the oil industry was down, we used our credit cards quite a bit; we didn't even think about it. We just kept using them and using them and realized we had incurred a tremendous amount of debt," Charlie said.

The family's attitudes toward money would change as drastically as their surroundings when Charlie's latest job change took them across the state of Texas, from the small city of Midland to the outskirts of Dallas.

Julia recalled the billboard that introduced them to Crown Financial Ministries.

"We were driving down Loop-820 and saw on the billboard of Richland Hills Church, 'Want to find out what God has to say about your money?'"

When she and Charlie attended the church service that Sunday, Julia pointed to the Crown announcement in the bulletin and told her husband, "This is why we're here."

One Crown life group and two years later, the Sizemores have reduced their debt by 30 percent; Julia is running her own Web design business; and the whole family has benefited from a shared responsibility in their finances.

"It's opened up a lot of lines of communication because all four of us are more aware of where we are financially," Julia said. "Now we all sit down, and if there's a need, we look at the need; or if there's something that we want, we start saving for that."

The Sizemores saw more stability in their lives when they gave God a bigger role in their career and personal financial decisions.

Living by God's provision has alleviated many sleepless nights for Charlie, who had always worried about the future. He'd like to help others find that same sense of peace about their finances. He's eager to help people cope with financial stress because he knows what debt and unemployment feel like. Charlie now serves as a Crown Money Map Coach Trainer.

"I primarily want to work with young couples to keep them from making the mistakes I made," Charlie said. "It never would have occurred to me, 22 years old with a college degree, that I needed to look to the Bible for financial advice."

For Charlie's family, changing bad spending habits did not come easily; it took both commitment and the grace of God.

"If we had not had Crown, we'd still be ignoring [our debt]," he said. "It took us 10 years to get there, and we've been working on it solid for three years now. . . . I think the first six months you're just changing habits. It's kind of like putting the brakes on and then you start moving backward."

Julia said they plan to be credit card free in three years and completely debt-free in 10 years. As they make steady progress, they are encouraged by God's blessings.

"If you're faithful with what you're doing, God takes care of you," Julia said. "Periodically, God sends us little checks. . . . We'll get a refund [that] matches exactly where we need to be in our budget."

Like her husband, Julia wants to share her wisdom with others. She serves on the Dallas/Fort Worth Crown City Team and has led the Crown Teen Study. Having applied the principles she learned in Crown to her own Web design business, Julia is leading a group of business women through Larry Burkett's study, *Business by the Book*. She is starting her company slowly, without accumulating debt, and donating her services to ministries.

In addition to finding more ways to serve, the Sizemores also have experienced the joy of giving. "Even though we are still on a very strict budget, we've been able to give more money than we've ever been able to give, and I've really enjoyed that," Julia said.

Charlie and Julia have already begun instructing their daughters in godly stewardship. For example, they required Lindsay and Kristen to participate in a Crown life group study before opening checking accounts, and they expect their daughters to print out budgets and balance checkbooks. Julia does not want her children to learn financial discipline the hard way.

"We've been through some very interesting times," she said. "But when you put it all in perspective, and you turn to God, you know that it's all okay. When you look back, God knew exactly what He was doing."

Action Steps

_____

_____

_____

_____

_____

_____

Celebration Plan

_____

_____

_____

_____

_____

7 WRAPPING IT UP WITH HOPE

So, would you like your spending plan to balance and to cover your needs? And would you like to buy a house or a car or some other major purchase in a prudent way—a way that allows you to rest comfortably without high-risk indebtedness? Good! You have more going for you than you might think.

There is much more to these equations than simple money math. That's just the surface. Beneath the surface is where you find true treasure. Beneath the surface is the heart of your greatest benefactor.

Don't make the mistake of thinking that this brief chapter is theological theory or that it doesn't speak to your needs in a practical way. This is as practical as it gets, because it deals with getting in the flow of God's will. No economic plan—including the perfect spending plan—can accomplish what you need the most.

What do you _really_ believe?

Do you believe God has more interest in your welfare than you do? As self-centered as we naturally are, it's hard to believe, isn't it? But it's the theme of His message to us throughout the entire Bible.

God's Spirit constantly strives to cut through our fallen perspective and give us a more accurate view of reality. He wants us to know that He's not holding out on us; He's holding out for us. Even the Ten Commandments were not given to us for His benefit; they were given to protect us!

Are you aware that God is watching over you with unfailing love and care? Consider this: _"...Your Father knows what you need before you ask Him"_ (Matthew 6:8).

It's a simple sentence, easy to glide over without reflecting on its importance to your personal situation. But gliding over what Jesus says is always a mistake. Think through it for a moment.

1. **The speaker, Jesus, is the creator of the universe.**
   "Through him all things were made; without him nothing was made that has been made" (John 1:3, NIV). His understanding and power are unlimited, His authority and credibility beyond question. If He had been a mere man, His statement would be as meaningful as the words of any prophet, but He was not a mere man. Reflect for a moment on the credentials of the one making the statement.

2. **The speaker, Jesus, knows the Father intimately.** His knowledge does not rely on the descriptions and testimonies of others; it is not a faith-based acceptance of something unseen and yet hoped for. He and the Father are one. *"No one has ever seen God, but God the One and Only, who is at the Father's side, has made him known"* (John 1:18, NIV).

3. **Jesus identifies the Father as "your Father."** He is not distant and uninvolved. Think of the most loving, perfect earthly father you can imagine—all he would do for the welfare of his children—and realize that he is merely a dim reflection of "your Father." God spared nothing, including His only Son, for you. Can you trust "your Father"?

4. **"Your Father knows what you need."** How could it be other-wise? Our inability to see Him causes us to doubt whether He is really there. Our inability to always get our way—to get instant gratification of our every prayer—causes us to wonder whether prayer really works, whether He is really listening, whether He really gets it. Jesus assures us that the Father gets it.

5. **"Before you ask Him."** Notice that Jesus never says we shouldn't ask. He doesn't conclude that our asking is unnec-essary; He merely emphasizes the point that the Father is so aware of our needs that He doesn't have to rely on us to inform Him. Our asking is an exercise for our benefit rather than for His education.

It's all about trust.

God uses money as an ongoing laboratory in our lives to increase our trust in Him—Whom we cannot see—over everything else, includ-ing money, which we can see—very clearly. Until we get to the place where we trust more in God's good provision than in our temporal trea-sures, He has to keep repeating the experiments—sometimes pain-ful—designed to open our eyes to His perspective.

Let your heart hear what Jesus pleads with His audience to see—not just in the abstract—but in the reality of their daily lives.

"Therefore I tell you, do not worry about your life, what you will eat or drink; or about your body, what you will wear. Is not life more important than food, and the body more important than clothes? Look at the birds of the air; they do not sow or reap or store away in barns, and yet your heavenly Father feeds them. Are you not much more valuable than they? Who of you by worrying can add a single hour to his life?

"And why do you worry about clothes? See how the lilies of the field grow. They do not labor or spin. Yet I tell you that not even Solomon in all his splendor was dressed like one of these. If that is how God clothes the grass of the field, which is here today and tomorrow is thrown into the fire, will he not much more clothe you, O you of little faith?" (Matthew 6:25-30, NIV).

We don't want to be people of "little faith," but we are naturally attuned to the limitations of our five senses. Unfortunately, our senses can never perceive the extent of God's reality even though creation reflects His splendor. Jesus continues his message with a clear implication: "Don't you get it? You can trust your Father to supply!"

"So do not worry, saying, 'What shall we eat?' or 'What shall we drink?' or 'What shall we wear?' For the pagans run after all these things, and your heavenly Father knows that you need them. But seek first his kingdom and his righteousness, and all these things will be given to you as well. Therefore do not worry about tomorrow, for tomorrow will worry about itself. Each day has enough trouble of its own" (Matthew 6:31-34, NIV).

True faith puts first things first.

Do you see the key? Verse 33 gives us God's perspective on life's equation. It's all about putting first things first. To put it in its classic propositional form, God is saying, "Look, I know this takes faith, but if you put Me first, I will take care of you. Period. And putting Me first means trusting Me, so stop worrying about what you can't control."

Putting God first means diligently following His direction to the best of our ability. We don't sit idly by, expecting Him to pull rabbits out of the hat and hand them to us. We act in accordance with His instructions. We work. We give. We save. We deal honestly. We repay our debts. We live the law of love. But then, having done our best to handle money—and every other part of our life—according to His direction, we rest in perfect confidence that He will provide for our needs and that He will never leave or forsake us. We plan, but we don't worry.

Jesus continues His message by driving the point:

> *"Ask and it will be given to you; seek and you will find; knock and the door will be opened to you. For everyone who asks receives; he who seeks finds; and to him who knocks, the door will be opened.*
>
> *"Which of you, if his son asks for bread, will give him a stone? Or if he asks for a fish, will give him a snake? If you, then, though you are evil, know how to give good gifts to your children, how much more will your Father in heaven give good gifts to those who ask him!"* (Matthew 7:7-11, NIV).

This is not a new message. Jesus was just delivering it in a new way and demonstrating it in His sacrificial life. It's an extension of a hope-filled directive from the Old Testament.

> *"Trust in the LORD and do good; dwell in the land and enjoy safe pasture. Delight yourself in the LORD and he will give you the desires of your heart. Commit your way to the LORD; trust in him and he will do this"* (Psalm 37:3-5, NIV).

If you want the desires of your heart—and who doesn't?—both the Old and New Testaments give us the same formula. "Trust…do good…delight…commit…trust."

Do a self-check.

How do you know if you're trusting? Jesus offers a simple test. *"So in everything, do to others what you would have them do to you, for this sums up the Law and the Prophets"* (Matthew 7:12, NIV).

You can't live the Golden Rule without trust, because sometimes you will suffer for it. It requires you to act independently of what you receive from others. You can't do that without believing that somehow God will deal with the injustices you will suffer.

Do you treat people as well as they deserve? If so, you fail the test. That's the standard by which the world lives. Jesus calls us to a radical standard, one that operates in dramatic contrast to the world's. Instead of merely treating people as *we* think they deserve—setting ourselves as their judge—we are to treat them as we *want* to be treated.

When you honestly follow the Golden Rule, your actions demonstrate your trust; when you do not, they betray any hollow declaration of trust in God.

Start fresh, with new hope.

Make it your goal to grow daily in faith, trusting God with everything that is dear to you. Trust and obey. Ask, seek, knock. Make your wishes known, committing your way to Him.

As you create and implement your spending plan and save for big-ticket purchases, remember to put first things first. God—not your employer, lender or retirement plan—is your Provider. *"...Your Father knows what you need before you ask him."*

> *"What, then, shall we say in response to this? If God is for us, who can be against us? He who did not spare his own Son, but gave him up for us all—how will he not also, along with him, graciously give us all things?"* (Romans 8:31-32, NIV).

Action Steps

_____

_____

_____

_____

_____

_____

Celebration Plan

_____

_____

_____

_____

_____

_____

SECTION THREE

INSURANCE AND INVESTING

This section will help you regardless of your stage of life. From teens needing car insurance to retirees needing to learn more about investment options—and everyone in between—you will find information to help you weigh important options.

Some people believe that having insurance or investments indicates a lack of trust in God. For them, it may. Some people also believe that seeking medical treatment indicates a lack of trust in God, and for them, it may. Although we do not judge them for their convictions, we do not share them.

At the same time, we recognize the constant temptation to put our trust in human devices rather than in God, and such trust is clearly misplaced. It's the "rather than" that creates the problem; it implies an "either-or" condition: Either we trust God to do something or we do it.

We believe this condition is unnecessary and that God expects us to take a "both-and" approach in our management of His resources: We both trust God to do something and we do it.

Consider these examples:

- Many Scriptures indicate that God will provide our needs, which Jesus emphasized in His sermon on the mount, particularly Matthew 6:25–7:12. But He also mandated that we work. God provides AND we work.

- He invites us to seek His wisdom, but He expects us to use the intelligence He gave us in making decisions. God gives wisdom AND we use our brains.

- He distributed money to three different men in the parable of the talents (Matthew25:14-28), but He expected them, as His stewards, to do something with it—to put it to work for an increase. God entrusts resources AND we manage them for growth.

- He cares for the poor and needy, but He expects us to participate in
meeting their needs (Matthew 25:31-46). God gives AND we give. God has not called us to passivity. Trusting Him does not mean lack of action on our part. James drives this point in his second chapter. Using Abraham as an example, he says, *"...His faith and his actions were working together, and his faith was made complete by what he did"* (James 2:22, niv).

How does this relate to insurance and investing? We should take responsibility to manage God's resources prudently while we trust Him implicitly for everything beyond our control. We act within the scope of what He has entrusted to us using the tools available to us.

We believe that insurance and investments are prudent management tools within the Master's expectation for our stewardship. We are also careful to keep them from eroding our complete dependence upon God, who alone is worthy of our trust. We look to Him for guidance, we act accordingly, and we trust Him for the results.

CHAPTER 8

INSURANCE

What Is Insurance?

In simple terms, insurance lets us pay a little now to cover future major expenses due to illness, death, accident, disaster, or theft.

Buying insurance is like storing grain for the winter months (Proverbs 6:6-8). Protecting ourselves against the cost of a catastrophic illness, which can devastate a family's finances, is a wise investment.

Unfortunately, insurance has become a means to "protect" against every possible contingency no matter how unlikely. This misuse of insurance can lead to greed, laziness, waste, and fear. But, worse than that, it can lead to dependence on insurance instead of on God, our ultimate provider.

Current Attitudes

Americans have developed an "insurance ethic" that often justifies cheating insurance companies. Some of the rationalizations include:

- Viewing the insurance company as impersonal. They don't really know anyone there, so it's not like they're cheating a real person. But an insurance company is comprised of employees, members/stockholders, policy holders, etc. When the company is cheated, all of these people suffer. As followers of Christ, we can live above this temptation by observing His command in Matthew 7:12: *"In everything, therefore, treat people the same way you want them to treat you."*

- Viewing the insurance company as wealthy. Many people believe the wealthy acquired their money dishonestly, making them fair game. Jesus enables us to overcome this judgmental attitude: *"Why do you look at the speck that is in your brother's eye, but do not notice the log that is in your own eye?...First take the log out of your own eye, and then you will see clearly to take the speck out of your brother's eye"* (Matthew 7:3, 5).

- Expecting too much from insurance—protection from any and every loss. No product can do this. Although God could protect us from every loss, He will not. To do so would not be in our best interest. Rather, He lovingly filters everything that occurs to us, guaranteeing that *"God causes all things to work together for good to those who love God, to those who are called according to His purpose"* (Romans 8:28).

- Desperation, brought on by fear. This may result from an emphasis on protecting rather than providing for the family. An obsession to protect every possession is a failure to recognize God's ownership—or at least a failure to internalize the comfort and peace His ownership offers. It is one thing to use insurance as a prudent steward; it is quite another to overburden our family's spending plan with inordinate insurance costs in an effort to protect our stuff. Throughout the Gospels, Jesus repeatedly encourages us not to fear or worry, assuring us that *"...your Father knows what you need before you ask him"* (Matthew 6:8).

Regardless of current attitudes, dishonesty is a violation of God's character. We must never rationalize it. God is ready to provide and bless your efforts in wonderful ways as you trust Him and demonstrate it by honestly doing the right things.

Biblical Perspective

If we understood and accepted our various responsibilities, there would be little need for insurance. When a family is in need, other families should respond. *"At this present time your abundance being a supply for their need, so that their abundance also may become a supply for your need, that there may be equality; as it is written, 'He who gathered much did not have too much, and he who gathered little had no lack'"* (2 Corinthians 8:14-15). Unfortunately, most are not at this point.

Insurance is most important in those situations in which a potential loss would be great. This is especially true when another's loss must be considered, as in automobile liability coverage. *"A prudent man sees evil and hides himself, the naive proceed and pay the penalty"* (Proverbs 27:12).

Choosing an Agent

Since your insurance agent will provide important counsel beyond your area of expertise, choose carefully.

1. As a first level of screening, ask the agent for references.

Second, check the agent's level of experience. Don't deal with a nonprofessional agent or one who sells insurance part time. Also check to see if the agent has earned a professional designation, such as CLU (Chartered Life Underwriter), ChFC (Chartered Financial Consultant), CFP® (Certified Financial Planner), CPCU (Chartered Property and Casualty Underwriter), or RHU (Registered Health Underwriter). These designations won't guarantee that a particular agent is best for you but, at the very least, they do show that the agent has completed a disciplined course of study.

2. Expect cooperation. Be sure your agent thoroughly analyzes your insurance needs. Don't tolerate an agent who tries to pressure you into buying more insurance than you can afford or need.

3. Proverbs 1:5 says that *"a man of understanding will acquire wise counsel."* When it comes to insurance, the source of wisest counsel should be a knowledgeable, experienced Christian agent.

The average novice in the area of insurance will need the very best counsel possible. Thoroughly read everything the company asks you to sign. If you don't understand it, require the agent or company to write it out in language you can understand.

Also be sure you understand your policy before you buy it. Find out how much coverage it provides and if it has any exclusions. Don't wait until you file a claim to find out what your policy covers.

Choosing an Insurance Company

One of the most important insurance decisions you must make is choosing an insurance company. After all, the timely payment of your benefits depends on that company's stability. Although there are many good insurance companies not listed in the "top 20," dealing with a company in the top 20 usually is best for the inexperienced person.

As you go through this process of choosing an insurance agent and company, pray as God's steward for His wisdom and direction.

Part 1

PROPERTY AND CASUALTY INSURANCE

Home Owner's Insurance

A *home owner's insurance* policy covers calamities that could happen to your home and its contents. It also covers liability from many things—fire, theft, hail. (Be aware that coverage for flood damage requires specific underwriting.) Usually, a home owner's policy is the least expensive way to insure a dwelling.

When you buy home owner's insurance, you need to be aware of the difference between actual cash value insurance and guaranteed [true] replacement value. Actual cash value refers to the depreciated value of the items; guaranteed replacement means your contents and structure will be 100 percent replaced. Guaranteed replacement is usually worth its small additional cost.

Dwelling Insurance

Dwelling insurance, although not as comprehensive as home owner's insurance, may be just as expensive. Because of age, condition, or location, some dwellings are not insurable under home owner's policies.

Renter's Insurance

Renter's insurance covers the value of your furniture and other possessions for replacement. It also provides liability coverage if someone is hurt as a result of your negligence or the negligence of your children. An example of this is someone falling over a toy or slipping outside of the home.

Umbrella Liability Insurance

An *umbrella liability policy* gives you extra coverage not provided by your auto and home owner's policies.

People with a large net worth or an occupation with a lot of public exposure may be wise to have additional coverage in our sue-happy society. It is more likely to be needed as the result of a car accident than an incident in the home, but an umbrella policy covers liability for a broad range of risks.

Automobile Insurance

Most states require *liability insurance* on all cars. This type of insurance covers the damage a driver might cause to others in an accident.

Everyone should carry at least liability insurance whether the state requires it or not. Potential liability is great, and the cost of liability insurance is relatively small.

One "at fault" accident can put a family in debt for life. Remember, *"The prudent sees the evil and hides himself, but the naive go on, and are punished for it"* (Proverbs 22:3).

Full Coverage

Full coverage on a vehicle includes all basic coverages: bodily injury, liability, property damage, medical payments, uninsured motorists, collision, and comprehensive.

Full coverage is worth considering on a newer car; some lenders even require it. It is often offered as part of the loan package, but it's usually best to buy it directly from the insurance company or agent.

Bodily Injury Liability

This pays for injuries to other people or for their death as the result of an accident involving your car. It covers people in other vehicles, guests in your car, and pedestrians, regardless of who is driving your car.

Coverage under this type of policy uses terms like "100/300." The first number is the amount in thousands that the policy will pay for one person. The second number is the amount in thousands that it will pay for all persons involved in an accident.

Property Damage Liability

This portion of the insurance policy covers damage to property caused by your car. Covered property includes such things as houses, buildings, fences, livestock, and any other property belonging to someone else.

The terms of coverage are expressed as "50/100/25." Each number represents thousands and is the maximum the insurance company will pay. The first number is the amount paid for each person injured; the second number is for each accident; and the third number is for property damage.

Personal Injury Protection

This will pay benefits to injured persons for medical expenses, lost wages, substitute services (if someone is unable to take care of his or her household), and death, no matter whose fault the accident was.

The protection is in effect whether a person is riding in or on your vehicle, getting in or out of it, or is struck as a pedestrian.

Medical Payments Coverage

This covers medical expenses that result from accidental injury to anyone riding in your vehicle or to anyone struck as a pedestrian.

Collision Insurance

Collision insurance pays for damages to your vehicle if you are involved in a collision. It does not cover the vehicles of anyone else involved in the accident.

Usually, a deductible is written with this coverage. And the company will pay only the market value of your car if there's an accident.

For example, suppose you have a six-year-old compact car with a market value of $1,000. You're involved in an accident that causes $2,500 in damage to your car. Instead of receiving $2,500 to fix your car, you would receive only $1,000 minus your deductible. If you had a deductible of $500, you would get only $500 ($1,000-500) to take care of the $2,500 damage.

You can see why it often does not pay to keep collision coverage on a car more than three years old unless it is a very expensive car.

Depending on your financial situation, you may be able to "self-insure" an older model car. Just set aside the value of the car into an interest-bearing savings account—to be used in the event your car is damaged.

Comprehensive Physical Damage Insurance

This provides for the replacement of glass and losses that result from anything but collision, such as fire, theft, vandalism, and hail. It is relatively inexpensive.

The cost of this coverage doesn't vary much with the car's age. Make the decision based on your budget. If the cost is very high for your income, carry liability only.

Uninsured Motorists

This covers injuries to you and your family caused by a hit-and-run driver or one who doesn't have liability insurance.

Other Coverages

Death and dismemberment insurance covers you or your family if there's a death or loss of a limb in an automobile accident.

Towing insurance pays part or all of the towing charges if your car breaks down.

Rental car reimbursement provides you with a car while yours is being repaired.

No Automobile Insurance—Faith or Foolishness?

Proverbs 27:12 has the answer to this question. It says, *"A prudent man sees evil and hides himself, the naive proceed and pay the pen-*

alty." If you don't look ahead to see the evil and protect yourself, you will end up paying a penalty.

In most states, driving without liability insurance is not just bad judgment; it's illegal. You can go to jail for it, and your house and car can be taken if you hit somebody and can't pay the damages.

If you choose to disobey the law, you are willfully disobeying both the law and God's Word. *"Every person is to be in subjection to the governing authorities. For there is no authority except from God, and those which exist are established by God"* (Romans 13:1).

Liability insurance protects those who might be injured as the result of an accident you caused. If your "living by faith" shifts the risk to others, you are not living by faith; instead, you're forcing them to accept risk for something that they shouldn't have responsibility. Make the choice to be a blessing to others, and God will bless your willingness to be kind and thoughtful in this way.

Automobile Insurance for Teens

Whether a teenager owns a car or not, the issue of insurance must be addressed. Almost every insurance company will raise parents' insurance rates as soon as their sons or daughters are 16 and become licensed.

Remember what Proverbs 29:17 says, *"Correct your son, and he will give you comfort; he will also delight your soul."*

Most parents use their teenagers to shuttle other children back and forth. If you do the same, you need to set some very fundamental rules for the use of the car, for buying the insurance, and for maintenance.

Don't wait until your children become teenagers to begin training them for this serious responsibility. By taking extra time with them and preparing early in their training process, you will have more peace of mind and more trust as they take on more responsibility.

How to Save on Automobile Insurance Costs

We've already seen that the age of your car and your ability to "self-insure" can reduce insurance costs. But taking advantage of discounts will also reduce cost.

Discounts are offered for:

1. good students with a B average or above

2. successfully completing a driver's education course

3. taking advantage of a carpool

4. multi-car families

5. students away at college

6. air bags

7. antitheft devices

8. senior citizens

9. farmers

10. defensive drivers

11. nonsmokers or nondrinkers

12. females age 30 to 64 who are the sole drivers.

You should check with your insurance agent to see if you qualify for any of these discounts.

It's also much cheaper for you to add a teenager to your insurance policy than to buy a separate policy. Limiting teenagers to a small percentage of the total use of the family car can lower your rates.

Anyone will save money by avoiding traffic violations. Speeding or ignoring traffic signs puts points on your driving record and adds dollars to your premiums.

In addition, the type of automobile you drive affects your premiums. If you drive a sporty or fancy car, you can expect to pay higher premiums.

Be sure to let your agent know immediately when circumstances change within your family. Review your coverage annually.

Other Types of Insurance Coverage

Long-Term Care Insurance

The majority of older people live in retirement homes or in their own homes because they are able to take care of themselves. But for those who need nursing home care, the expense can be enormous.

The cost of *long-term care (LTC) insurance* must be weighed against your ability to pay the premiums and the probability that you'll need such insurance.

If an indigent person needs nursing home care, the state will care for him or her with our tax dollars. But the Lord says we are to honor our fathers and mothers.

The word "honor" implies financial help. The long-term solution for our society is for us to take care of our older family members (1 Timothy 5:8).

Remember, if you can't afford insurance, then you have to believe God will take care of your needs another way.

Since *LTC insurance* is a relatively new field, treat it with even more care than you would give to other kinds of insurance. Search the Internet using the words "long-term care insurance" for current information.

The Consumer Law Page (http://consumerlawpage.com) contains plentiful advice, concluding that "long-term care policies are only for people with significant assets. . . ."

They also warn that very high commissions for LTC insurance policies result in pressuring vulnerable seniors to buy policies they cannot afford to maintain, noting that "far too many policies are cancelled by policyholders on fixed incomes as they grow older and their premiums increase accordingly."

Perhaps most sobering are these lines: "If you cannot afford to hire a lawyer to interpret the contract you want to buy, you should ask yourself if you can afford to buy coverage and, once you are in poor health and look forward to receiving policy benefits, whether you then will be able to pay for a lawyer to enforce your rights under the contract if benefits are not forthcoming. . . . Despite the claims of sales personnel, most policies are so flawed that if agents were honest about the policies' limitations, many customers would probably not purchase them at all."

Funeral and Burial Insurance

The best plan in existence to reduce burial costs is called the Funeral Consumers Alliance. When a family member dies, the Alliance guarantees burial at a very low cost.

The plan offered is through a standard funeral home. For more information, visit their Web site at funerals.org.

A second way to reduce burial costs is to visit your local funeral home in advance of death and prepay the funeral expenses. If you have a burial plot and pay for it before death, the cost is much less.

A third way to reduce burial costs is to donate your body to a medical school. The medical school will use the corpse for experiments and will provide burial at no cost.

Part 2

HEALTH AND DISABILITY INSURANCE

Today, health insurance is a basic need. Few families can afford the cost of even one hospital stay. So, medical insurance represents good, logical planning for most of us. It also makes good health care possible for families that otherwise couldn't afford it.

Health insurance is too complex to be discussed thoroughly in this book, and significant changes in the health insurance industry are taking place. Consult a professional for advice if your family is not covered by a plan provided by your employer.

Managed Care Plans

In recent years we have seen a major movement to *managed-care-type plans*. The goal of these plans, which are offered by many insurance companies, is to cut costs by negotiating a reduced charge with physicians and hospitals. These plans are more commonly known as Health Maintenance Organizations (HMOs), Preferred Provider Organizations (PPOs), and Point of Service plans (POSs). As managed care continues to evolve, we will see many variations of these managed care plans.

Health Maintenance Organizations (HMOs)—HMOs negotiate with major employers to take care of all their health care needs—from surgery to minor care. But the employers must use the HMO's doctors, hospitals, and clinics.

Preferred Provider Organizations (PPOs)—PPOs are similar to HMOs from the standpoint of negotiated charges. The main difference is that you can choose the physician you want to see. There are member and nonmember physicians and hospitals. If you choose a member provider, then your out-of-pocket expenses will be less than if you choose a nonmember provider.

Point of Service Plans (POSs) —These plans allow an insured person to choose his or her primary physician. This physician will have agreed to discounted fees for services rendered. The insured then would have to see this physician for all ailments first in order to receive the highest discount. If the insured decides to see a specialist on his or her own, the out-of-pocket expenses will be greater.

Medicaid

Medicaid pays medical bills for low-income people who can't afford the costs of medical care. It is a government-sponsored program with strict guidelines for eligibility. To find out if you qualify, contact your local public health or welfare office.

Medicare

Medicare is a government sponsored health insurance program for people who are 65 or older. Some disabled people also qualify.

It is a two-part program. Part A provides hospital benefits for short-term illness. It also provides some benefits for care in a skilled nursing facility or at home.

Individuals 65 or older who don't qualify for Medicare can still receive it by paying a monthly premium, which is adjusted each year.

Part B of Medicare is optional medical insurance, which is available for a small fee each month. You may have the premium automatically deducted from your Social Security benefit check, if you receive one. Part B pays most of your medical and surgical fees. It is an excellent value because it is so inexpensive.

Is Medicare Supplemental Insurance a Good Buy?

Medicare supplemental insurance is designed to take up where Medicare leaves off. It is relatively inexpensive for the amount of coverage it provides.

A good supplemental insurance policy should cover the whole range of health problems. Using a number of policies to cover specific illnesses is usually more expensive.

When buying health insurance, be sure your agent lists all preexisting conditions. This will help you avoid being disqualified if you file a claim.

Your supplemental policy should provide for long-term custodial care, such as nursing home care or care at home. In addition, it should give you the option of using facilities other than those approved by Medicare.

Also look for a shorter deductible period and a shorter waiting period for preexisting conditions. As always, compare policies and prices before you buy anything.

What If You Can't Afford Insurance?

This is a major concern when it comes to any type of insurance—but especially health insurance. Some people aren't covered by a group health plan, and they can't afford an individual plan or major medical plan. Their basic needs have to be met by God's people. This doesn't mean God can't provide, but He sometimes provides through His people.

If you don't have insurance at work and can't afford to buy it yourself, consider doing the following. Look for an inexpensive major medical plan with a high deductible that will pay for catastrophic illnesses. You may consider taking this plan to your Christian employer and asking if the company will pick up the cost.

If not, go to your church fellowship and present the plan as a legitimate need. If they don't respond, then you and your spouse should pray about it and decide if you are where God wants you to be.

Another option is to pay your own medical and dental bills. Many medical professionals will be happy to work something out with you. You may be able to clean their offices or find another way to work off what is owed. Do not avoid or run away from medical bills. God will help you find a way to handle them.

Summary

When planning your health insurance program, be sure the coverage fits your needs and your budget. Examine your policy carefully. Know which expenses are covered by your insurance and which are not.

Don't duplicate coverage. Some companies won't pay if you have another policy for the same coverage.

Look over your policy every year to be sure it fits your family's current needs. Be sure you are covered against major expenses when funds are limited. Compare policies and costs. They vary greatly from one company to another.

Disability Insurance

Psalm 37:25 says, *"I have been young and now I am old, yet I have not seen the righteous forsaken or his descendants begging bread."*

Maintain a balance when buying insurance. Trying to insure yourself against every contingency can rob your family of needed funds and the blessing of God's provision. Still, the possibility of being disabled and unable to work is a situation you should address.

Depending on your level of disability, you may qualify for disability benefits from Social Security. Like other Social Security benefits, disability is based on the amount of Social Security taxes you've paid into the system.

Among all Social Security programs, disability is one of the most complicated. Therefore, it would be wise to become more familiar with the program by obtaining a free copy of the booklet, *Disability*, from your local Social Security office (SocialSecurity.gov).

Many employers provide a form of disability protection through a group plan. Find out if your employer offers this coverage.

In summary, pray about this decision and trust Him to show you the answer for your specific situation. He cares deeply for your well-being and wants the best for you and your family.

Part 3

LIFE INSURANCE

The purpose of *life insurance* is to continue providing for your dependents if you die. A reasonable calculation of their needs will reveal a target amount of insurance benefit that your policies should provide.

The Benefits of Owning Insurance

Most primary wage earners in a home need the greatest amount of life insurance when they're young—especially if they have a spouse and children at home who probably couldn't support themselves after the death of provider.

Insurance is used to produce the needed income; in that way it becomes a substitute for the breadwinner. To repeat Proverbs 27:12, *"A prudent man sees evil and hides himself, the naive proceed and pay the penalty."* The insured is looking ahead, seeing a potential problem and providing for it before it occurs.

Second, insurance frees surplus funds. Let's assume that the primary wage earner makes $35,000 a year. If this person dies, the family will need a $35,000 income. Let's further assume that Social Security will provide $15,000 a year for dependent care. The family is still $20,000 a year short. Where will the funds come from? It would take about $340,000 in assets, invested at 6 percent, to provide the $20,000 that the family still needs to survive.

These funds can be provided by saving $340,000, in which case insurance is not necessary, or by purchasing life insurance.

Even if a couple has $340,000, they may want to use the money to buy a home or for other purposes. If so, buying insurance would free the money for other use.

The Liabilities of Owning Insurance

One liability of insurance is that it costs money: You must reduce current spending to provide for the future.

Another liability of insurance is that it can divert your dependency from God. Solomon wrote, *"Trust in the Lord with all your heart and do not lean on your own understanding. In all your ways acknowledge Him, and He will make your paths straight"* (Proverbs 3:5-6).

This doesn't mean we must avoid insurance, but it does mean that God, not insurance, should be the object of our trust. Choose to trust God first as you make decisions about insurance, knowing that He will guide your decisions. Your salvation and relationship in Christ is your greatest insurance policy!

Term Life Insurance

Term insurance provides coverage for a specific period of years. This period of years is known as a "term," and when the term ends coverage must be renewed.

Most term policies do not build any cash reserves, but they provide the greatest amount of death protection for your dollar. Term insurance is strictly for protection. In order for it to pay benefits, the policy must be in effect when you die.

Term premiums are based on age, with the cost going up as you get older. If you're going to buy term insurance, remember these four things.

1. Buy only what you need.

2. Be sure the policy is renewable to at least age 90.

3. Be sure it won't be canceled due to your bad health.

4. Compare its cost for a 20-year period to other kinds of insurance, such as whole life.

If you find that term insurance is best for your needs, seek counsel about the various policies before buying one from a professional Christian insurance agent.

Cash Value Insurance

Cash value insurance is known by a variety of names, including whole life, universal life, variable life, single premium life, and variable adjustable life. It is usually purchased for an individual's lifetime and, as more and more premiums are paid, the policy builds cash value.

Interest is earned on the cash value, just like money invested in a bank. Many times the policy also will pay dividends (cash returns), which can be used to offset the cost of insurance.

The most basic type of cash value insurance is **whole life**. A young person buying whole life, or some other type of cash value insurance, would pay higher premiums than for term insurance. However, one benefit of some cash value policies is that the premium never changes.

For young families on a tight budget, cash value insurance can be a major expense. At worst, it can be so costly that these families don't buy enough coverage at a time when their need is greatest.

Universal Life

Universal life is sometimes called "complete" and "total" life insurance. It is known by various names, including adjustable life and flex life. Universal life is a combination of term insurance and a tax-deferred savings account that pays a flexible interest rate.

That interest rate usually reflects current market rates. Therefore, it will be much higher than the savings rate of traditional insurance policies.

Universal life is broken down into three parts:

1. the death benefit,
2. administrative costs, and
3. the savings portion of the policy.

Some agents emphasize the savings you will accumulate by age 65. These agents are promoting the investment side of the plan. But, be sure the policy meets your primary goal, which may be maximum death benefit rather than accumulation.

Stated returns on your universal life policy will not begin to show until you have been paying premiums for 15 to 20 years. If you cancel the policy before this time, it will cost you dearly, compared to buying term insurance and investing the difference in a tax-deferred vehicle.

Variable Life Insurance

Several types of insurance, including universal life, whole life, and adjustable life, may also take the form of a *variable life insurance* policy.

A variable life policy is considered a security and is sold by prospectus. The death benefit and cash value go up or down depending on the investment vehicles chosen inside the policy. A variable life policy offers loan privileges, optional riders, and surrender and exchange rights, just as any other cash value policy does.

These new policies offer higher returns, but they also mean greater risk for policyholders. Returns can change drastically from year to year.

Sometimes the product that suits your needs best is actually a combination of things. That's what you get with variable life. It combines traditional insurance provisions with flexible administrative procedures. It also has investment features that compare with other market investments.

The Concept of Survivorship Life Insurance or Second-to-Die Life Insurance

Thanks to the Economic Recovery Tax Act of 1981, a husband and wife can postpone estate taxes until after they both die. This is done through a provision known as the Unlimited Marital Deduction.

This provides couples with increased flexibility during their lifetime. But in many cases, it places a substantial tax burden on their estate and its beneficiaries.

Survivorship life insurance is designed to address this need. Unlike traditional life insurance, which covers the life of one person, survivorship life covers two lives, with proceeds payable at the second death.

Reducing your estate tax burden is not the only use for a survivorship life policy. Other uses include the following.

- Key person insurance. This would apply to cases in which an employer could self-insure or absorb the loss of one key individual but not two.

- Business buyout. One example of this is the purchase of a family business from aging parents. A child working in the business owns the policy on the parents.

- Charitable gift replacement. This provides heirs with replacement cash when assets are used to fund a Charitable Remainder Trust.

Is Insurance a Good Way to Save?

One argument for cash value policies is that they "force" you to save money. After all, you must pay your premiums to keep the policy going, and the more you pay the more you save.

As a short-term investment, the savings in most insurance policies draw less than half the interest that can be earned elsewhere. It is a high price to pay for a lack of discipline.

Proverbs 19:20-21 tells us, *"Listen to counsel and accept discipline, that you may be wise the rest of your days. Many are the plans in a man's heart, but the counsel of the Lord, it will stand."*

Conclusions

A good way to determine the type of insurance you need is to consider two things:

1. the amount of insurance you need, and
2. the amount you can afford to pay.

Obviously, you need to consider the current annual cost of a policy. But you also need to consider the cost of that policy during the next 20 years.

Shop for the best policy that fits your individual needs at the lowest cost. The best value usually comes from buying term insurance and saving the difference in a deferred or tax-free investment.

Unfortunately, most people don't save the difference; they spend it. At the same time, their term insurance premiums increase as they grow older. Eventually, these premiums may become too expensive for them to afford.

In conclusion, term insurance plus savings provides the best value. However, if you haven't been disciplined enough to save the difference by age 35, convert to a whole life plan.

How Much Insurance Is Enough?

"There is a grievous evil which I have seen under the sun: riches be-ing hoarded by their owner to his hurt" (Ecclesiastes 5:13). It's very important, especially for young families with children, to determine the proper amount of insurance for their needs. Among the considerations:

- The ages of your children. The younger they are, the longer they'll need to be supported if you die.

- The income capability of the surviving spouse. This is a major factor, particularly if that spouse is not working.

- Existing debts, current lifestyle, and any other sources of after-death income.

One person may want to supply enough insurance so that his or her family can live on the interest income. Another may wish to provide enough for a specific number of years. These decisions are important and should be made together by husband and wife.

A typical family's insurance needs begin when the first child is con-ceived. Those needs reach a maximum amount when the last child is conceived.

Another period when there's a greater need for insurance is when the children are grown and out of the home but the surviving spouse has not reached 62 years of age.

Unless he or she is disabled, the spouse won't qualify for Social Security survivor's benefits until age 62. Even then, the benefits will be reduced, because full benefits aren't paid until at least age 65.

If the spouse qualifies as disabled (based on Social Security's definition of "disabled") he or she can receive survivor's benefits as early as age 50.

The Life Insurance Needs Worksheet at the end of this chapter will help you determine an appropriate amount of insurance for your family situation.

Budgeting for Insurance

Once you've decided how much insurance you need, you must decide how much you can afford. Insurance should take no more than 5 percent of your Net Spendable Income (NSI). Net Spendable Income is the amount you have left after you've paid your tithe and taxes.

The 5 percent figure above does not include house or automobile insurance. It does include life insurance, health insurance, and disability coverage. Still, a 5 percent allotment for all these insurance needs is not very much. But we're assuming that you have health insurance as part of a group plan. Many people receive group health coverage through their employers, who pay a portion of the premiums, thereby reducing the cost to the employees.

If you're not part of a group health insurance plan, this percentage of your budget will increase, and you'll have to be very "choosy" about your life and health insurance plans.

If you increase the insurance area of your spending plan from 5 to 10 percent, then there is no alternative but to decrease another area to keep the total of percentages at 100.

Should Both Spouses Have Life Insurance?

In many families, both husband and wife are equal or nearly equal wage earners. When a family depends on both salaries, both spouses probably need to be insured. If one died or became injured, the family would be in deep financial trouble, possibly losing their home, cars, and virtually everything else they own.

If funds are limited, efforts should first be made to insure the primary wage earner. However, if there is a sufficient amount of money, insuring both husband and wife should be considered.

Should Children Have Life Insurance?

There are two logical reasons to have insurance on your children:

1. for burial expenses, and

2. to guarantee that they will be insurable in later years.

However, the only necessary reason is burial expenses. Making your children insurable is not usually necessary, since only a small fraction of people are uninsurable at the time they marry.

Things to Avoid When Buying Life Insurance

There can be a big difference between buying what you need and buying what an agent wants to sell you. So, if you're in the process of buying life insurance, consider the following advice.

1. Avoid the double indemnity clause, which pays double if you die in an accident. This is an extra expense for something you probably won't need. Most people die from causes other than accidents. If you're counting on double indemnity to provide enough insurance, you're gambling with your family's future. You should be sure you have enough insurance, regardless of how you die.

2. Forget premium waivers that pay your premiums for you if you become permanently disabled. They represent a large expense for a very small benefit.

3. Don't be pressured into buying insurance. Don't put it off un-necessarily, but take the time to learn what you need and what will provide the best value.

Pointers for Policyholders

1. Keep your company informed of your address. Each year a number of policyholders move without notifying their insurance companies. When you do this, you're taking a chance on hav-ing your policy lapse.

2. Read your life insurance policy. Your agent should be willing to help you. Be sure you understand the basic provisions and benefits.

3. Keep your policy in a safe place. You can get a duplicate policy if yours is lost or destroyed by fire but not without some incon-venience and delay.

As an additional safeguard, keep a separate record of your policies. Be sure that your beneficiary knows where a copy of your policy is kept. Generally, policies must be sent to the company when you file for benefits.

4. Discuss your insurance program with your family or other beneficiaries.

5. Review your life insurance program with your agent once a year or when a major event occurs (birth, death, marriage, divorce).

No Insurance

God may direct some people not to have life insurance or any other after-death provision. However if you're married, both the husband and wife should agree on this decision—after they've prayed together and sought God's peace. If you have any doubts, go ahead and buy the insurance. You can always cancel it later.

Credit or Mortgage Life Insurance

Credit or mortgage life insurance is sold in connection with home, auto, or other credit extensions. It is the same as decreasing term insurance, which offers a steady premium but declining benefits.

This type of policy is designed to relieve survivors of economic strain by paying off the outstanding loan balance of the deceased. Credit disability insurance also covers monthly payments if you are disabled.

This is a relatively expensive form of insurance. Unless you are in a high-risk, hard-to-insure category, you're better off to increase your regular insurance to cover any mortgages or loans you have.

Final Note

This information is designed to cover basic biblical principles that apply to insurance. For more specific information, contact a Christian insurance agent in your community. In the event of any disputes or irregularities, you may contact your state insurance commissioner's office for assistance. And don't hesitate to contact Crown, particularly if you have questions that go beyond product and technical issues that are best answered by your agent or broker; and, we will refer you to someone who can answer your questions and concerns.

Just-in-time Insurance Avoids Double Loss

Grant and Lori Hudson

Grant and Lori Hudson lived in Air Force base housing (no rent or utility costs) on an officer's salary. Assured of a stable income, they spent freely. Ten years later they owned a house but had also spent their way to a $17,000 credit card balance.

Unfortunately, this was not their only problem. While Grant was away on a long deployment, Lori's need for emergency kidney surgery and a legal issue regarding the sale of their house left them with an empty savings account, $62,000 in debt, and no house.

When Grant returned home from his deployment, he went to a financial counselor, who advised him to file for bankruptcy. But a friend introduced the couple to Crown Financial Ministries. They called for help and applied many of the biblical principles from the materials they purchased.

Lori and Grant worked out a repayment plan with their creditors and avoided bankruptcy, relieving some of their stress. This was a blessing, because Grant began to have problems with his job. He was passed over for a promotion to the rank of major on two occasions and finally accepted a contract with the Air Force that allowed him to continue as a captain with a severe salary cut. Still, with God's help, he and Lori continued to repay debt, build a savings account, and build a college account for their children.

Five years later, Grant's aunt passed away and left part of her estate to him. As a result, the couple received an unexpected check in the mail that covered the entire balance of their debt.

Things had definitely improved, but Lori was concerned about their insurance. "My husband had not been a believer in insurance," she says, noting that he only had a $50,000 life insurance policy through the Air Force. "He would get testy if I tried to discuss it with him."

But one day, while driving down the road, Lori and Grant tuned in to the Crown's radio broadcast and heard them talking about insurance. "I can remember sitting in that passenger seat and saying, 'Lord, please let him hear this!'" Lori says. "I had prayed so hard about it." Grant, however, seemed to pay no attention to the message and said nothing about it to Lori.

Within less than a month, Grant suffered a fatal aneurysm in the parking lot at the base after a late-night flying mission.

When representatives from the base arrived at Lori and Grant's house the following morning, one of their first questions was, "Did he have insurance?"

Lori didn't know, but Grant's commander was certain that Grant had provided for his family. "That man told me a month ago that he'd heard a radio broadcast about insurance and financial planning," the commander told Lori. "I know that man took care of you."

The commander ordered two men to conduct a search, and they found that only 17 days before his death, Grant had increased his insurance from $50,000 to $200,000.

"Crown taught my husband how to love his family in life," Lori says, "and how to love us at death."

Today, one passage of Scripture that is very precious to Lori is Psalm 27:13-14. It illustrates how God has worked in her life and met her needs. *"I am still confident of this: I will see the goodness of the LORD in the land of the living. Wait for the LORD; be strong and take heart and wait for the LORD"* (NIV).

You don't have to know it all!

This volume of information may seem overwhelming—more than you ever wanted to know. Don't worry: You don't need to grasp it all immediately, and you never have to become an expert unless it's your occupation.

The combination of this basic insurance information and the biblical principles that apply to it will enable you to make wise decisions for the welfare of your family. Make prayer the centerpiece of your decision-making process. *"Be anxious for nothing, but in everything by prayer and supplication with thanksgiving let your requests be made known to God. And the peace of God, which surpasses all comprehension, will guard your hearts and your minds in Christ Jesus"* (Philippians 4:6-7). God's peace is more valuable than anything we could ever buy.

Action Steps

_____

_____

_____

_____

_____

_____

Celebration Plan

_____

_____

_____

_____

_____

_____

Life Insurance Worksheet

Date _____

GROSS MONTHLY INCOME   **Sample**

Present annual income needs:	$ 53,280
Subtract deceased person's needs:	$ 9,000
Subtract other income available: (Social Security, investments, retirement)	$ 10,000
= Net annual income needed:	$ 34,280

Net annual income needed, multiplied by
12.5 (assumes an 8% after-tax investment
return on insurance proceeds): $ 428,500

LUMP SUM NEEDS

Debts:	$ 8,000
Education:	$ 20,000
Other:	$ 0
Total lump sum needs:	$ 28,000

TOTAL LIFE INSURANCE NEEDS: $ 456,500

GROSS MONTHLY INCOME

Present annual income needs:	$ _____
Subtract deceased person's needs:	$ _____
Subtract other income available: (Social Security, investments, retirement)	$ _____
= Net annual income needed:	$ _____

Net annual income needed, multiplied by
12.5 (assumes an 8% after-tax investment
return on insurance proceeds): $ _____

LUMP SUM NEEDS

Debts:	$ _____
Education:	$ _____
Other:	$ _____
Total lump sum needs:	$ _____

TOTAL LIFE INSURANCE NEEDS: $ _____

Once you have quantified your approximate life insurance needs, deduct the amount of your present life insurance coverage to determine whether you need additional life insurance. Then analyze your spending plan to determine how much new insurance you can afford. Seek counsel to decide the precise amount and type of insurance that would meet your needs and spending plan.

CHAPTER 9 INVESTING

Part 1

TEN KEYS TO SUCCESSFUL INVESTING

Tom Hunter was a well-known Christian leader who believed God had given him a revelation about how to solve America's oil problems. It was 1980, at the height of the Arab oil embargo, and commuters throughout the nation were feeling the pinch of skyrocketing prices at the gasoline pump.

Tom claimed that he had been approached by an angel who revealed the location of hidden American oil deposits. These deposits, in an area where no oil had ever been discovered, defied all geological patterns established by the petroleum industry.

Despite the evidence contradicting his claim, Tom remained convinced that his revelation was true. He set out to raise the $3 million needed to drill in this spot, beginning with $50,000 from people in his church to do a prospectus and brochures.

He wanted to offer stock in the venture but was unable to obtain the necessary registrations. In Tom's opinion, satanic forces within several state governments had blocked the registrations. So, he offered stock anyway. With the help of two associates, Tom was able to raise nearly $600,000 from Christians who heard about the oil-drilling venture. Several families borrowed against their homes, and one 80-year-old couple risked their entire savings in the project.

The hole was dry and all the funds were lost. Lawsuits flew like snowflakes as disgruntled Christians sued one another, in violation of Paul's teachings in 1 Corinthians 6. The media picked up on the lawsuits because many elderly people had been duped into investing. As a result, the cause of Christ suffered disgrace in many communities as the venture's promoters were prosecuted, convicted, and given prison sentences.

These weren't stupid people—neither the promoters nor the investors. And they were probably no greedier than average; the promise of unusually high returns influences many to throw money at speculative ideas without careful research. Most of them—particularly the older investors—hoped for enough gain to achieve peace. That was their first mistake.

More money is not a bad thing, but it is not the source of peace. True peace comes only from God. *"Peace I leave with you; My peace I give to you; not as the world gives do I give to you. Do not let your heart be troubled, nor let it be fearful"* (John 14:27).

Find the Right Balance

Investing is not unscriptural. In fact, in the Parable of the Talents (Matthew 25:14-30), God gave to the stewards according to their abilities and directed them to manage their portions well. Each was rewarded or punished according to his stewardship.

We should distinguish between investment performance and investment purpose. Performance will vary based on our response to constantly changing factors beyond our control. Increased knowledge and discipline should lead to increased skill and better performance.

Investment purpose, however, is not a matter of skill; it is a matter of intent. This is the foundation for the spiritual and moral side of the equation. As you learn to invest money according to God's principles, you'll find that God will increase your opportunity to help other people. That, in reality, is the true purpose of godly investing: to increase your assets so that you can serve God more fully.

Allowing material assets to erode through bad management is not good stewardship. It's a sign of laziness and poor stewardship. But if you simply multiply and store assets without purpose, you'll be guilty of hoarding—like the rich fool in Luke 12:16-21.

The 10 keys to successful investing are common principles that provide a solid foundation for any investor regardless of differing needs.

Key 1: Formulate Clear Investment Goals

No one should invest without having an ultimate purpose for the money. Whether it is for education, starting a business, retirement, etc., you should have a clear financial goal. Let's look at some common goals.

Retirement Goal

Even if you plan to continue working past 65, you may not be able to be as productive at that age. If you have to take a job that pays less than you need to live on, you'll need retirement savings to supplement your income. If you have enough in your retirement account to provide all the income you need, your work choices do not have to be dictated by financial necessity. Instead, they can reflect your heart and passion.

If your retirement goal is to someday sit down, kick up your heels, and do nothing, we would recommend a better goal. We believe it is beneficial to remain active after 65, especially when you have the freedom to work as a volunteer for a nonprofit or Christian organization. Our Christian service doesn't end at 65. In fact, retirement years provide outstanding opportunities to advance God's work.

We recommend becoming debt-free, including your home mortgage, as your first investment goal in preparing for retirement. Once you've achieved that goal, you will be in a stable position to accelerate other investment vehicles.

The exception to this would be a company retirement account that matches your contributions. This benefit is too good to pass up if you can possibly afford it. Contribute up to the maximum amount your company will match, and allow any additional surplus in your spending plan to go toward mortgage reduction.

With your home paid off, you can start preparing for retirement and/or your children's college education with the money you were paying each month on your mortgage.

It takes discipline to invest this money, but it makes sense. You can't depend on Social Security to be your sole retirement plan; it was never intended to be anything more than a supplement to your retirement income.

Proverbs 6:6-8 says, *"Go to the ant, O sluggard, observe her ways and be wise, which, having no chief, officer or ruler, prepares her food in the summer and gathers her provision in the harvest."* It may seem that the "harvest" years of your life will stretch on forever, but remember that the winter years are coming. God will provide the means to save for the future as you trust Him.

Education Goal

Unlike those who are trying to preserve a windfall, a couple planning for their children's education may have to think more in terms of growth. This depends on the amount available to invest and the time in which it can be invested.

Let's assume, for instance, that a couple can put aside $1,000 a year for the education of their children, who will reach college age in about 10 years. With an interest rate of 5 percent and an inflation rate of 3 percent, at the end of 10 years they will have a little over $12,000. This will not be enough to educate one child, much less two or three. They will need to take some additional risks to achieve the growth they require.

This is the principle of "risk versus return," and we'll be dealing with it again and again. The higher the rate of return you need, the greater the degree of risk you'll have to assume.

Growth Goal

Some people need more growth potential in their investments. But there are others who seek a lot of growth potential because they're hoping to get rich quick. These people are willing to take big risks in an effort to become rich overnight. But Proverbs 28:22 says, *"A man with an evil eye hastens after wealth and does not know that want will come upon him."*

Tax Shelter Goal

This goal is very complex. Tax laws constantly change, and the average investor has few shelters left beyond depreciation and interest.

Beware of the common perception that paying interest is a good tax shelter. When you pay interest to save income tax, you lose and the lender gains.

On the other hand, depreciation and investment tax credits can be legitimate tax shelters. But an important principle to remember is that when you "defer" income tax through depreciation, you eventually must recapture it. Most tax shelters don't really eliminate income tax; they only defer it to a later time.

Key 2: Avoid Personal Liability

Many get-rich-quick schemes, as well as many tax shelters, are available only if you accept personal liability for a large debt. God's Word warns against "surety," which means making yourself personally liable for indebtedness without a sure way to repay.

For example, suppose you wanted to buy a piece of property for $10,000 but had only $2,000 as a down payment. You put your $2,000 down on the property and then sign a note for $8,000 that says, "If I can't pay the note, the lender has the right to recover the property and sue me for any deficiency." Although the note is not likely to use these exact words, the fine print generally contains the described provision. This is surety.

On the other hand, let's assume you buy the same $10,000 piece of property with the same $2,000 down payment, and sign a different note for $8,000. This one reads, "If I can't pay the note, the lender has the right to recover the property and keep what I've already paid, but I owe nothing additional."

The second note involves no personal liability for any deficiency. The legal term is *non-recourse* or *exculpatory* debt, meaning you have limited your liability to the collateral at risk. This avoids surety because you always have a sure way to pay: surrendering the property.

Avoid personal liability. Then, if you buy equipment, property, or investments, the most you can lose is the money you have "at risk," not future earnings. Failure to do this can result in the total loss of all your family's assets. Investments that go bad often do so during the worst times in the economy, the very times when you are least capable of carrying the loss.

Illustration. *Ron and Stan were doctors who invested together in numerous real estate ventures. One of these investments was an apartment complex, which had been offered for about half of its appraised value. The deal had required a $1 million mortgage with a minimal down payment of only $50,000.*

Both men were assured that there was no way the investment could go bad. After all, they could make money with the complex only 50 percent occupied, and it had never been less than 80 percent occupied. The only hitch was that they had to personally endorse the note. In other words, they personally guaranteed the lender against any losses.

About two years later it was discovered that the complex had urea formaldehyde insulation in the ceiling and walls. It was condemned, and health officials required that the entire structure be torn down.

The insurance paid for a portion of the loss, and Ron and Stan were able to sell the land for another portion. But they were still personally liable for nearly half a million dollars. Ron went bankrupt. Stan, who was a Christian, felt it would not be right to go bankrupt and committed to repay the loan.

The investment itself was good—barring the unknown health hazard—and the deal was excellent. The problem was that Ron and Stan entered into surety by signing for personal liability. Remember the wisdom of Proverbs 22:26, which says, *"Do not be among those who give pledges, among those who become guarantors for debts."* Don't enter into surety, no matter how good the deal sounds.

Key 3: Evaluate Risk and Return

An important factor in investing is called the "risk versus return" ratio. The higher the rate of return, the higher the degree of risk. You can lower the risk by education and careful analysis, but you cannot eliminate it.

The reason an investment pays a higher rate of return is because it must do so to attract the needed capital. For example, an insured CD or a government note may pay 3.5 percent, but a corporate bond may pay 5.5 percent to 10.5 percent.

Why does a corporate bond pay a higher interest rate than a government note? Because the risk in corporate bonds is higher than in government notes. Before investing in anything riskier than an insured savings account, you need to ask yourself this fundamental question: "Can I really afford to take this risk?"

The answer to that question normally depends on two factors: age and purpose. The older you are, the less risk you can afford to take because it's more difficult to replace the money.

If the purpose of the money is for retirement or education and both are still years away, you can probably afford to take a higher risk.

However, if you need the investment funds to live on right now, then you need the lower risk, regardless of age. If you find an investment that promises a high rate of return with a low degree of risk, watch out; there's no free lunch.

As Proverbs 14:18 says, *"The naive inherit foolishness but the sensible are crowned with knowledge."*

Key 4: Keep Some Assets Debt Free

If you're using leverage (borrowed money) to fund some of your investments, keep at least 50 percent debt free. This also assumes you are following the guidelines of Key #2 and are not accepting surety. In other words, the money you have at risk in the investments is all you can lose. You have no contingent liability.

The basic idea behind this strategy is to leverage about half of your investments, expecting that the investment earnings on the money you borrow will be greater than the interest rate you pay to borrow it.

If you leverage no more than half of your investments and you lose them due to an economic downturn, the other half remain sound— provided you haven't entered into surety with the leveraged ones. Leveraging is better suited for experienced investors who know what they're doing. Even then, the risk can be high. It's not a good idea for the average investor, who doesn't have a large surplus.

Illustration. *Joe was a real estate developer whose business had suffered a large slump due to the economy in his area. He had no surety and had kept at least half of his assets debt free. This would enable him to sell his leveraged investments without losing everything.*

Joe's friends encouraged him to take their approach and sell some of his debt-free investments to help carry some others. He had tens of thousands of dollars in the other investments and didn't want to lose them.

His friends were risking good assets to feed their debts. They had very little choice, since they had personally endorsed every loan and everything was at risk. But Joe had a choice.

He was about to gamble that the economy in his area would turn around before his assets were exhausted. A wise counselor advised against risking good assets to feed loans. "If they can't pay their way or be sold, let them go," he said.

Joe followed this advice and is still in business, but most of his associates have failed. In fact, he was able to develop a new business: managing properties for insurance companies and banks that have foreclosed on heavily indebted real estate.

Key 5: Be Patient

How many investments have you seen advertised as really bad deals? Although bad ones abound, they all look good initially. And since most salespeople sincerely believe in their products, it's up to you to sort out the good from the bad. In your eagerness to get your money working for you, remember that patience will help you avoid many errors.

You must know what your goals and objectives are and only select the investments that help you meet them. Remember that greed and speed usually work together, which is why most get-rich-quick schemes require quick decisions. Let patience be your strong ally in defeating greed's bad choices.

It helps to recognize the strategies employed by get-rich-quick schemes. They all:

1. Attract people who don't know what they're doing. When you invest in areas that you know little about, it's difficult to evaluate a good or bad investment. Christians are often very gullible and prone to follow the recommendations of other Christians who don't know what they're doing either.

2. Encourage people to risk money they cannot afford to lose. Most people are more cautious with money they've earned than with money they've borrowed. Borrowed money comes so easily that it's easy to risk.

3. Pressure people to make investment decisions on the spot. Many get-rich-quick plans rely on group meetings and a lot of emotional hype. But if you hear of a deal that sounds so good that you don't want to wait and pray about it, pass it up. Good investments are rare and seldom flashy.

Illustration. Chad was a young computer salesman who reluctantly called Larry Burkett for counsel after his wife, Chris, pressured him into it. Here is Larry's account of the story.

"We have to see you right away," he said. "I've got a deal that's too good to pass up and I've got to move quickly." We scheduled a time for the following day.

When they arrived, Chad talked about a computer hotshot in Colorado who had developed a program to do stock market trades between the U.S. and European stock exchanges. Profits would be made on the differences between the two markets.

This "specialist" was taking investors and making over 10 percent per month for them. Chad had already cashed in his retirement plan and was about to borrow against the equity in their home. He calculated that he could make enough to start his own business in just two years.

Chris was panic-stricken at the thought of Chad risking $25,000 with someone he didn't even know. But Chad said he had talked with several other investors who were making lots of money. He said the software developer had paid exactly what he promised every month.

We asked, "Why does he need your money if he's able to make over 100 percent per year? Why doesn't he just borrow the money at 10 percent per year instead of paying out 10 percent per month?"

Chad answered, "He wants Christian investors so he can get into other ventures in the future."

Since any investment targeted primarily at Christians is worthy of some suspicion, we asked Chad if he would mind us checking out this person.

"No," he said, "but how long will it take? I've got to make a decision quickly or the opportunity will close."

Our counsel regarding biblical principles and get-rich-quick schemes fell on deaf ears. Chad had already made his decision. This appointment was just a necessary step to pacify his wife.

Our investigation found nothing on this computer trading genius. If he had learned his trade by handling stocks and bonds, nobody knew about it. We called to get a financial statement and were repeatedly assured that one was "on the way." But we could never get even the slightest documentation on what he was doing.

In the meantime, Chad invested $25,000 in this venture and received a $3,000 check for the first month's profits. The next month he was offered the option of reinvesting the profits, which he did over our objections. But when the third month rolled around, Chad's distribution never came.

The state securities commissioner impounded all the assets of the "trader," pending an investigation for securities fraud. He had not been trading stocks at all. He'd simply been raising money from gullible people—a lot of them.

The system was pretty simple—a classic Ponzi scheme. He paid dividends by raising more money each month. Once investors had received a month or so of distributions, they were "allowed" to reinvest their profits, which most did.

As long as the circle of investors kept expanding, the trader had no problems making the payments—and a huge profit. His only overhead was a computer to keep up with the payments.

The end came when an investor tried to talk his brother-in-law into investing. Fortunately, the brother-in-law was a security investigator who knew a scam when he saw one.

By the time this "stock trading" operation was shut down, it had raised more than $20 million and had a list of clients that read like who's who in entertainment, sports, and business.

As the Proverb says, *"A faithful man will abound with blessings, but he who makes haste to be rich will not go unpunished"* (Proverbs 28:20).

Get-rich-quick schemes always look great at the outset. If they didn't, no one would buy them. Be cautious and patient. *"Rest in the Lord and wait patiently for Him"* (Psalm 37:7). Before you do anything, talk about it, pray about it, investigate it, and give God time to answer.

Key 6: Diversify

The old adage that says, "Don't put all your eggs in one basket" certainly applies to your investment strategy.

Let's assume, for example, that you have $1,000 to invest and you want to buy some stock. If you put your $1,000 into one company's stock, then all of your money rests on how that one company's stock performs.

A good alternative is a mutual fund, where thousands of investors pool their money to buy stock in many different companies. This gives you immediate diversification.

You can achieve further diversification by splitting your investment into different areas of the economy. Real estate, gold and silver, stocks and bonds, CDs—all of these offer some advantages.

The probability is that when one of these areas is down, another will be up. So rather than having to sell the one that's down, you could sell one that's up.

Remember that Bernard Baruch said, "When everybody else is buying, it's time to sell." What you should strive to do is buck the trends, rather than be forced to go with them.

The current proliferation of mutual funds and exchange-traded funds (ETFs) enable you to diversify in ways that would have been impossible a few years ago. But don't make the mistake of thinking that owning shares of several mutual funds automatically means broad diversification. If the funds don't differ significantly in their investment strategy— the kinds of stock they hold—you could end up with several copies of the same thing. We'll talk more about mutual fund diversification later.

It is important to remember that the principle of diversification is not a one-time decision. In other words, we don't diversify and then forget it. Managing God's assets is a lifelong privilege and responsibility. If we lack knowledge, we should try to gain it. Spending an hour a day for six months studying any area of investing will teach us more than many investment salespeople know.

Key 7: Consider Long-range Bonds

Your investment program should take into account long-range economic trends, especially inflation. People who follow only short-range trends often get trapped.

When the economy is doing well and inflation and interest rates are down, people want to jump into the stock market and "make a lot of money." Some of them will make a lot but then panic during a short-term downturn and lose most or all of it.

People who speculate may wind up losing more than they made, especially if they borrow to invest. When the market drops, they can't afford to ride it out, so they sell in a down market, guaranteeing losses.

It is always important to take the long-term approach; whatever is going on right now will eventually reverse. Long-term thinking does not mean that your investments remain stagnant, but it does mean that you resist panic. Bernard Baruch noted that "most people tend to panic when their assets decline in value, and they will sell simply because they have not taken a long-range view of things."

Inflation and the government's attempts to control it are the most significant economic trends that affect investments.

The most inflation-proof investments over several decades have been real assets: things that you can use and touch, such as land, metals, apartment buildings, or houses—and stocks or funds that focus on real assets.

During periods when inflation and interest rates are down, many of the paper investments like stocks and bonds do very well. During this time, people tend to forget about inflation.

That can be a costly mistake in a debt-run economy. When inflation turns around and interest rates increase to combat it, years of growth can be wiped out in a few months.

Key 8: Focus on What You Own

Many people with significant net worth have been wiped out during economic downturns. We've counseled many who had looked great on paper but had highly leveraged assets requiring regular payments. When interest rates rose and the economy tightened, they couldn't keep up with the payments, and they lost everything, including their homes.

Illustration. Here's another account from Larry Burkett. Even in today's economy, you'll see that the only things that really change in these classic stories are the names, dates, and figures. History has a way of repeating itself!

We met an oilman in the late 1970s. He was a committed believer and a member of the Christian Oilmen's Association. He had gotten into the oil business just before the oil embargo and had seen the price of oil go from about $6 a barrel to over $30.

It seemed that everything he touched turned to gold, and he was thoroughly hooked on the Christian "prosperity message." He literally believed that his giving guaranteed him immunity from economic problems.

He was worth millions through oil leases and several drilling operations, but everything was leveraged to the limit. He used every increase in oil prices to borrow more against his reserves so that he could expand further.

When we challenged him on the principle of surety, he became very defensive and ducked behind the normal Christian escape: "God told me to do it."

He said he prayed regularly about every decision. Furthermore, he believed every increase in his assets was evidence that God was confirming his actions.

To make matters worse, he had adopted a good-economy mentality, believing that the economy would continue to inflate indefinitely and carry oil prices with it. He failed to realize that much of the inflation was due to increasing oil prices, which couldn't rise indefinitely.

Everything changed in the early 1980s, when the oil cartel fell apart and oil prices dropped. Newly elected President Reagan used high interest rates to curtail the money supply and bring inflation under control.

At the same time, higher oil prices encouraged worldwide conservation efforts that began to reduce the demand for oil. This triple blow crippled the oil industry.

Established companies like Shell, Texaco, and Gulf did well with their pre-inflation oil leases. But most of the new ventures got wiped out, including this Christian oilman.

He could have cashed out in 1979 with perhaps $20 million; yet in 1986, he saw his home and furnishings auctioned off by the court.

When we say focus on what you own, we mean what you own that is liability free. Highly leveraged assets may produce stunning returns over short periods of time when conditions are perfect, but they become time bombs when conditions change. Make it your goal to have at least half of your assets free of any debt. If you can't do that right now, make it your number-one long-range goal.

How can you do it? By saying, "The next time I sell an investment, I'll use the proceeds to pay off another investment." As the Lord said, *"For which one of you, when he wants to build a tower, does not first sit down and calculate the cost, to see if he has enough to complete it?"* (Luke 14:28).

Key 9: Know Where to Sell

Before you buy, always know where you can sell the investment. This key is very important when you're dealing with "exotic investments," such as gemstones, silver, gold, or collectibles.

You can do very well buying these items if you know what you're doing. But most people who buy collectibles have no idea of where or how to sell them.

For example, suppose that the precious metals market is doing very well and you want to sell an antique silver plate. Let's arbitrarily assume that silver is being quoted at $16 an ounce.

The first thing you discover is that your plate is probably worth a lot more than its silver content, based on what you paid for it as an antique. So the price quoted on silver has little meaning.

The market for your plate would be a collector and, normally, through an antique broker. Many novice collectors have discovered to their dismay that the price they paid for an object was retail—or more—and the price they're offered is wholesale—or less.

Let's assume that you bought gold in bullion form. Unless you have an agreement with the sales company that they will buy it back from you, you may have a difficult time finding a buyer.

If you decide to sell it, and gold is being quoted for $800 an ounce, you will discover that a broker won't give you $800 an ounce for it.

In fact, he may offer as little as $700 an ounce even though it's certified bullion. Why? Because he needs to make a commission on it too.

Other collectibles, such as figurines, paintings, stamps, and coins, are very difficult for a nonprofessional to sell profitably.

When you invest in these you need to have a clear understanding of how and where you can resell them. We've counseled many people who said, "Well, the salesperson told me that if I ever wanted to resell, he would buy it back."

But later they found that their salesperson was no longer around. Even businesses that have survived for 50 years can still fold, especially in a bad economy. It is vital to know you have a ready market without unacceptable transaction costs.

Usually investors are better off staying with less exotic investments that have multiple markets available.

Key 10: Train Family Members

Every family member should be trained in the principles of sound investing. This is critical for children because they'll eventually move away and be responsible for managing their own family's finances.

It's critical for wives because 85 percent of them will outlive their husbands. That's an important statistic to remember when developing an investment portfolio. People who don't understand investments often sell at the wrong time and suffer significant losses. Also, since it is not uncommon for a husband and wife to die together in an accident, the older children should be brought into decisions involving investments. At a minimum, leave instructions so they'll be able to manage your portfolio without having to dispose of it just to pay estate taxes after your death.

Part 2

DEVELOPING AN INVESTMENT STRATEGY

In order to gain a thorough understanding of the principles of investing, a few definitions are in order.

First, both income and growth may be included under the general term "return." In other words, you may have cash income from a certificate of deposit (CD), or you may have growth income from a rental house. Both are considered "return" on investment. The first is immediate and the second is long-term.

Income is the average current yearly yield. Growth refers to average yearly appreciation. So, if you get a 5 percent cash return from a rental house after all expenses are paid, and the house is also appreciating 5 percent per year, it has a 10 percent per year return on investment.

The term "risk" refers to potential loss. In other words, what is the probability that you will get your money back on an investment? Risks are numerous and vary with the type of investment. Let's use the relatively low-risk example of fixed-income securities. With this type of investment, the major sources of risk include the following.

1. **Interest rate risk.** Changes in interest rates can affect bond returns and bond prices.

2. **Purchasing power risk.** Over a period of time, inflation eats away at your purchasing power. The more severely inflation rises, the more severely your purchasing power is diminished.

3. **Market risk.** The market (in general) affects the price behavior of your securities.

4. **Marketability risk.** How easily can you sell a particular issue at or near prevailing market prices?

5. **Business risk.** If the issuer has large financial and operating risks, the risk of default is increased.

6. **Reinvestment risk.** This is your ability to reinvest your principal and/or coupon/ dividend receipts at a desirable rate.

7. **Call risk.** Your security may have a call feature that gives the issuer the right to prematurely retire the obligation. As a result, you may be forced to reinvest the funds in a lower-yielding investment.

8. **Price risk.** This particular risk is based on changes in interest rates. Depending on the maturity of your obligation, price behavior may be affected to a lesser or greater extent. The longer it takes your obligation to mature, the more susceptible you are to this type of risk. Therefore, short-term obligations have less exposure to price risk when interest rates are rising.

In this section, we'll present some of the more common investments available and place them on a multi-tiered system. These investments are tiered according to *risk* and *return (income)*.

We have assigned a scale from 0 to 10 that can be applied to each type of investment. Zero represents the least risk or the least return, and 10 represents the highest risk or highest return.

Therefore, an investment with a return potential of 0 and a risk factor of 10 would represent the worst possible investment.

An investment with an income potential of 10 and a risk of 0 would be the best possible investment. (Unfortunately, they don't exist.)

We also have added a third factor: *growth*. Growth means the ability of an investment to appreciate (grow in value, such as common stocks).

Investments such as bonds have a potential growth factor also. If a bond pays a yield of 10 percent and interest rates drop to 8 percent, the bond value increases. If interest rates increase to 12 percent, the bond value decreases, resulting in negative growth or loss of capital.

We'll cover these five tiers:

1. Secure income investments
2. Long-term income investments
3. Growth investments
4. Speculative investments
5. High-risk investments

The ratings you'll see on the following investments represent an opinion, not an absolute fact. Times and economic conditions constantly change, and the degree of return or risk for most types of investments will fluctuate accordingly.

When interest rates and inflation are high, real property, residential housing, apartment complexes, or office buildings generally do well. But when interest rates and inflation are down, stocks and bonds generally do well.

Unfortunately, high and low are relative terms that are best gauged in the rear-view mirror—after it is too late to respond with certainty. And much of the time, interest and inflation are neither particularly high nor low; they are somewhere in the middle, trending in a direction. If you could guarantee even the direction in advance, the market would provide easy money, but market direction is never uniform or orderly. It is characterized by so many sudden changes that no daily chart is predictable. Line up 10 different experts and you'll get 20 plausible scenarios.

Tier 1: Secure Income Investments

Government Securities

(Income 5)(Growth 0)(Risk 1)

Treasury bills (T-bills), U.S. savings bonds, series E bonds, and Series I bonds all fall into this category. You can also buy shares of mutual funds that invest exclusively in T-bills or Ginnie Maes.

Bank Securities
(Income 5)(Growth 0)(Risk 3-4)

One advantage of bank investments like savings accounts, certificates of deposit (CDs), and insured money funds is that you can invest with smaller amounts of money; you can purchase a CD for as little as $500. The disadvantages are that they offer little or no growth because the payout is fixed and the income is taxable as it is earned.

Be certain that you invest with a bank or savings and loan protected by the FDIC or a credit union insured up to $100,000. In a worst-case scenario, the government will print the money to pay what it owes.

If you elect to tie up your money long-term and have a choice between a government security or bank note, the government security includes the safety of being a primary obligation of the government.

Money Funds
(Income 4-5)(Growth 0)(Risk 2-8)

Money funds are the pooled funds of many people. The funds are used to purchase short-term securities. These are not true savings accounts but are short-term mutual funds that pay interest.

Money funds are available through most brokerage firms, savings and loans, and banks; those offered by brokerage firms aren't federally insured against losses. Interest rates usually are adjusted monthly.

It's important to verify the rating of any money fund frequently. If the rating drops below "A," remove your money and select another fund.

Also, don't maintain more than $25,000 or 10 percent of your assets (whichever is lower) in any one money fund.

Tier 2: Long-Term Income Investments

Municipal Bonds
(Income 5)(Growth 0)(Risk 7-8)

These are bonds issued by a local municipality, usually a larger city like Houston or Hartford. The primary selling feature is that most or all of the income from municipal bonds is exempt from federal income tax (and state income tax in the state where they are issued).

The disadvantages of individual municipal bonds are: (1) they have low yields; (2) they normally require a large initial investment; and (3) there may not be a readily available resale market for them.

Mortgages
(Income 8)(Growth 0-5)(Risk 3-4)

A mortgage is a contract to lend someone money to buy a home or other real property. The lender (investor) holds the mortgage rights to the property until the loan is totally repaid.

One way to become a mortgage holder is to buy a mortgage through a mortgage repurchase agreement. These agreements are commonly offered by commercial lenders who want to resell loans they have made.

The seller normally discounts the mortgage to yield from 1 percent to 3 percent above the prevailing interest rates. So, if current interest rates on CDs are 7 percent, you can earn 8 percent to 10 percent through repurchased first mortgage loans.

The risk on this type of investment is relatively low because you have real property backing the loan. If a borrower fails to pay, you can foreclose on the property, but that requires a process beyond the interest and experience of average investors.

An important factor is the value of the property securing the mortgage. High-powered investment banks have lost billions through properties appraised at unrealistic prices and secured by high mortgages to unqualified buyers.

Corporate Bonds and Bond Funds
(Income 6-8)(Growth 0-3)(Risk 5-6)

A corporate bond is a note issued by a corporation to finance its operation. Quality bonds often yield 2 percent to 3 percent higher interest rates than an equivalent CD or T-bill.

The amount of return depends on the rating of the company issuing the bond. Bonds are rated from a low of C to a high of AAA. The higher the grade of the bond, the lower the rate of return, but the risk is lower as well.

Unfortunately, the rating of a company can change quickly. Most average investors would be better off using a bond mutual fund to achieve the long-term income they seek. The returns are slightly lower, but the risks are lessened through diversification in many companies' bonds.

Insurance Annuity
(Income 3-4)(Growth 0)(Risk 5-6)

This investment requires a prescribed amount of money to be paid into the annuity, and then the issuing insurance company promises a monthly income after retirement age.

The advantages of investing in annuities are as follows.

1. The earnings are allowed to accumulate, tax deferred, until you retire.

2. The investment is fairly liquid, so if you have to get your money out, you can, although there is often a penalty.

3. Compared to other tax-sheltered investments, the returns are good.

Be aware that the stated yield of an insurance annuity isn't necessarily what you will receive. Sometimes the percentage given is a gross figure from which sales and administrative costs are deducted.

It's best to ask for a net figure to do your comparisons. Get all quotes in writing from the agent offering the annuity.

Dividend-paying Stocks

(Income 4-5)(Growth 0-10)(Risk 6-7)

Common stocks usually pay dividends based on the earnings of the company. One advantage is that stocks can be purchased for relatively small amounts of money.

It's possible to invest in a stock paying a dividend of 7 percent to 8 percent and invest less than $100. This obviously appeals to the small investor. Since the dividend is totally related to the success of the issuing company, I would look for a company that has paid dividends for many years, particularly during economic hard times. Be aware, though, that just because a corporation has paid dividends for decades doesn't necessarily mean that it can continue to do so.

As stated previously, a good quality mutual fund can lessen the risk but achieve the same results. Professional management, together with broad diversification, provide a great advantage.

Tier 3: Growth Investments

This tier is in the middle and represents the crossover from conservative to speculative investments. During one cycle of the economy these investments may appear to be conservative, but then during the next cycle they could appear to be speculative.

Undeveloped Land

(Income 0-2)(Growth 6-7)(Risk 7-8)

During the highly inflationary '70s, farmland and other undeveloped properties were good investments. People speculated in land just as they did in income properties. This drove prices up and, unfortunately, tempted farmers to join the speculators.

The 1980s saw inflation subside and land prices level out. Consequently, raw land prices also fell. This scenario can and will change again as the economy changes in the future. Be sure that you find a trusted professional in this field to advise you.

Housing
(Income 5-7)(Growth 0-5)(Risk 3-4)

Housing costs are out of the price range of most average young couples, and since they have to live somewhere, most of them will rent, at least temporarily.

One advantage of investing in rental housing is that it can be done with a relatively small initial down payment. When investing in rental properties, the most important principle to remember is to assume no surety. If the house won't stand as collateral for its own mortgage, pass it by.

Rental housing not only generates income but also shelters much of that income through depreciation and interest deductions on taxes.

On the other hand, there are several negatives to consider before investing in rental housing.

1. If you don't want to be a landlord, don't buy rental housing.

2. If you have to pay someone to maintain and manage your properties, you give up a significant portion of the return.

3. It's not always easy to get your money out if you need it.

An alternative to investing in single-family rental housing is to invest in duplexes and triplexes. If you don't have the money to get into a duplex or triplex by yourself, there are two alternatives.

- You can invest in limited partnerships offered by individuals who purchase and manage duplexes and triplexes. Remember, however, that the managing partner has total control.

- You can invest with another person.

The advantage of owning a duplex or triplex is that your income isn't limited to one renter. With a single-family home, if your renter moves out, you have a 100 percent vacancy. But with a duplex you would still have 50 percent occupancy.

The liabilities with duplexes and triplexes are that they require a bigger investment and more maintenance, and you really do become a property manager.

Remember the three key factors about buying any rental property, whether it is a single-family house, duplex, or triplex: location, location, and location.

Mutual Funds

(Income 6-8)(Growth 4-5)(Risk 4-5)

A mutual fund is an investment pool for many small investors. A group of professional advisors invests for them, usually in the stock or bond markets.

There are specialized mutual funds that invest in precious metals, utility companies, government securities, and so forth. In fact, you can find a mutual fund for almost any area in which you want to invest.

Mutual funds are valuable for the small investor for several reasons.

1. You can invest with a relatively small amount of money (many mutual funds require as little as $500).

2. Your money is spread over dozens to hundreds of companies.

3. The return on the best mutual funds has averaged more than twice the prevailing interest rates for any 10-year period.

Potential investors in mutual funds should go to independent sources to check out the fund first. Since we are discussing growth mutual funds, it is important to verify the track record and projected earnings of any fund you might select. A prospectus from the mutual fund company will clearly define the "secure" or low-risk funds and the "growth" or speculative funds.

We prefer no-load (non-commission) funds because they don't subtract 5 percent or more from the initial investment. If the performance of commission funds were substantially superior to no-load funds, the commission would be a non-issue. But the best no-load funds compare very well. Still, all funds have annual expenses that cut into the return. Make sure you evaluate these expenses (often 1 to 2 percent) as well as any penalties you will incur if you buy and sell shares too frequently.

Tier 4: Speculative Growth Investments

Common Stocks/Aggressive Growth Mutual Funds

(Income 2-8)(Growth 0-7)(Risk 7-8)

Again, the advantages of common stocks are that you can invest with a relatively small amount of money and the potential exists for sizable growth. The liabilities of common stocks are obvious.

First, you can suffer a loss as easily as you can make a profit. Second, stocks require some monitoring to maximize their potential. Buying and selling requires broker fees, although many discount brokers will execute computer trades for $7 to $15 per trade.

Discount brokers and computer trading have removed the liability of high commission costs and replaced it with a new liability: the lure of over-trading. When stock investing moves toward day trading, it becomes less investing and more gambling. Many people have lost large amounts of money through impatience and trying to score quickly.

Generally, it is more profitable and much less time consuming to use top-rated no-load mutual funds. If you want a fund that mirrors the Dow Jones Industrial Average or some other index, there are many such index funds from which to choose.

If you want one that will perform exactly opposite of the DJIA or some other index—rising when the index falls and vice versa—several are designed to do that. Just be aware that they will lose money most of the time because bull (favorable) markets generally last much longer than bear (unfavorable) markets.

Precious Metals
(Income 0)(Growth 0-8)(Risk 8-9)

As mentioned before, precious metals such as gold, silver, or platinum can be purchased either for long-term growth or pure speculation. For long-term growth, buy the metal, put it in a safety deposit box, and hope it appreciates over a period of time.

Most people do this primarily as a hedge against a potential calamity in the economy. A small percentage of your assets invested in precious metals can help to balance other assets more vulnerable to inflation.

Remember Bernard Baruch's advice, "When everybody else is buying, it's time to sell." Especially when it comes to precious metals.

Finally, keep a long-term mentality about precious metals—at least those you invest in as a hedge. And remember that gold and silver fluctuate with the economy. Gold usually cycles faster and further than silver, primarily because more people trade in it. In general, the cycles of gold run opposite the U.S. dollar; so, for clues to the price of gold, watch the dollar's trends.

Other speculative investments include limited partnerships, syndications, penny stocks, and collectibles. It is virtually impossible to assign a rating to these since they vary so greatly, depending on the investor's expertise. Suffice it to say that the risks are great and so are the potential returns.

The reason that many of these investments are shown in both the speculative and high-risk categories is because they fall into either, depending on what the economy is doing at the time.

Tier 5: High-Risk Investments

These investments should play only a relatively small part (5 percent to 10 percent at the most) in any investment plan. Their primary value is the potential appreciation; in other words, speculation. Most generate little or no income and are highly volatile.

Gold and Silver
(Income 0)(Growth 0-10)(Risk 9-10)

Not only can you invest in precious metals for long-term growth, but you can also invest in gold and silver for short-term speculation. This would be most beneficial in a highly volatile economy where major changes were occurring.

Obviously, such events are difficult to predict and are extremely risky. They are only for the investor with a strong heart and cash. Unless you are a professional investor, this probably is not an area in which you want to risk much money.

Oil and Gas
(Income 0-8)(Growth 0-10)(Risk 10+)

In the late 1970s and early 1980s, when crude oil prices cycled up, oil and gas investments were the hottest things going. But many people who invested money in oil and gas did not understand the risks involved, and the vast majority lost their investments when the prices fell and marginal wells became unprofitable.

A high degree of risk exists, particularly in oil exploration. In an effort to reduce that risk, many people invested in oil and gas limited partnerships in known gas and oil fields. Not only did they lose their money on these investments, but they also discovered they were liable for environmental damages caused by the wells.

This kind of an investment is not only very risky but usually very expensive. Again, a glance back at the volatility of the economy over the past several decades gives us insight to current issues and "opportunities."

If you plan to invest in oil and gas, risk only a small portion of your assets, and don't let anybody talk you into risking larger amounts.

Commodities Market

(Income 0)(Growth 0-10)(Risk 10+)

Commodities speculation requires a relatively small dollar investment and can bring huge returns, primarily through the use of leverage.

Commodities are appealing, since a $1,000 investment in the commodities market can control $10,000 worth of contracts—or more—for future delivery. But remember: "A fool and his money are soon parted."

Investing in commodities is probably the closest thing to gambling that most Christians ever try. Actually, it is gambling. You can lose everything you own and even more. Commodity prices can move quickly above or below your initial investment, possibly triggering a forced sale that could result in losses exceeding your initial investment.

Collectibles

(Income 0)(Growth 2-10)(Risk 10+)

Antiques, old automobiles, paintings, figurines, and so forth are all collectibles that can be used while you hold them to sell.

One of the most important prerequisites to investing in collectibles is knowledge. You need to know value before investing. Second, you need to put some time and labor into locating the best places to buy and sell. Third, you must have the capital to wait for just the right buyer. Often, novice investors get discouraged and sell out at a loss.

Unless you have a high degree of knowledge in this area, the risk is inordinately high. With most items like antiques, automobiles, figurines, and paintings, you can develop the expertise you need by talking with other people and reading key periodicals. The rate of return on collectibles can easily be 10+, but the risk of loss is just as great.

Precious Gems

(Income 0)(Growth 0-4)(Risk 10+)

Diamonds, opals, rubies, sapphires, and other stones can be purchased for relatively small amounts of money. Then they can be mounted into a ring or pendant and worn while you're waiting for them to appreciate. The pleasure of wearing them may be the highest return you will ever see.

For every person we know who made money in gems, we know a hundred who lost money. It's almost impossible for a novice to know the true value of a gem, even with a "certified" appraisal. Worst of all, it's very difficult to sell gems at a fair price unless you have your own market. The rule here is to stay with what you know or with someone you thoroughly trust.

Limited Partnerships

(Income 0-7)(Growth 0)(Risk 10+)

Limited partnerships are formed to pool investors' money to purchase assets, usually in real properties. The investment is managed by a general partner who has the decision authority for buying and selling.

Since your investment in a limited partnership is no better than the property and the management, the key is to know the general partner's credibility.

A limited partner's liability normally is limited to the amount of money invested. Limited partnerships that carry contingent tax liabilities or require subsequent annual payments or operating loss guarantees should be avoided.

In the past, limited partnerships in properties, such as apartment complexes, office complexes, or shopping centers, were purchased primarily to shelter ordinary income.

But since 1987, most of these benefits have been gradually eliminated, and the tax write-offs can be used only to shelter passive income. For most investors, the risk is too high and the returns too uncertain.

Summary

This basic review of the five major types of investments is by no means an exhaustive review. However, it should provide you with a starting point for an investment strategy after you have developed a surplus in your spending plan.

There are many good materials available on the Web and in most public libraries, including books on investing. Always remember that balance is the key. Be careful about whose advice you take, because so many people are dedicated to the leverage principle.

Evaluate the risk involved with any investment. The higher the promised return, the higher the degree of risk, and the only way you can lower the risk is through your own personal expertise. You have to know what you're doing.

Part 3

ON-THE-JOB INVESTING

One of the best accumulation strategies in the world is a company-sponsored retirement plan. Whether they are called "401(k)" or "403(b)" plans, the names simply refer to the sections of the tax code that authorize company-sponsored retirement plans.

The investments available through a company retirement plan may be the same as those you would choose if you were investing on your own. Depending on the plan and how it is administered, your options can include annuities, mutual funds, company stock, CDs, or any combination of these.

The disadvantage of company retirement plans is that the selection of options you have to choose from is determined by the plan administrator(s). As a result, these options may or may not be the best available to meet your personal goals.

One large advantage of a qualified company retirement plan is that the funds you invest are tax deferred. In other words, taxes are not paid on the money until it is withdrawn. Many companies also offer matching funds, based on a percentage of what you choose to invest.

The sooner you start in a retirement plan, the less risk you will have to assume in order to reach your financial goals.

Your company will provide complete information on the options you have available under any company-sponsored retirement plan. Don't hesitate to ask for help in making the best choices for your specific situation.

Individual Retirement Accounts

The Economic Growth and Tax Relief Act of 2001 has significantly increased the amounts that may be contributed to both traditional IRAs and Roth IRAs. You can contribute to both an IRA and a Roth IRA as long as your combined contributions do not exceed an allowed amount for the year.

Married couples can each have an IRA and contribute up to the limit even if only one of them is employed. The non-working spouse's IRA is referred to as a spousal IRA and is funded by the working spouse. This is true for both traditional and Roth IRAs.

Traditional IRA contributions (within the limits) are tax-deductible. They grow tax-free until withdrawal and are fully taxed when withdrawn.

Roth IRA contributions are not tax-deductible, but they have the advantage of being tax-free when they are withdrawn—including the untaxed gains! Several other relaxed restrictions make Roth IRAs a very wise choice to complement other retirement plans.

Taxpayers age 50 or over who have earned income can contribute an additional amount over and above the regular contribution limit.

1. **Traditional IRA**—Currently, if an individual or spouse is an active participant in a qualified employer-sponsored retirement plan, the IRA deduction amount is phased out over certain adjusted gross income levels and varies based on different filing status categories. If your adjusted gross income (AGI) falls within the Phase Out range, you are allowed to make a prorated contribution that diminishes as you reach the No Deduction limit.

2. **Roth IRA**—The contribution* limit is reduced for incomes within a Phase Out range.

Qualified distributions from Roth IRAs are not taxed:

- if such distributions are made at least five years after the contribution was made and are taken after age 59½,
- in the event of death,
- in the event of disability,
- when used for buying a first home, or
- when used to pay higher education expenses.

Roth IRAs also have the advantage of not requiring withdrawals at any age as opposed to traditional IRAs that require them (along with paying the resulting taxes) at age 70½.

In addition, the tax advantages of a Roth account make it a great estate asset. An inherited Roth can give your beneficiary substantially more value than an equal amount of normal after-tax dollars.

---

* **DEDUCTION vs. CONTRIBUTION** – The **traditional IRA** uses the term "deduction" in its income-based limits rather than "contribution" because the two terms are definitely different. If your income exceeds the amount that allows you to deduct a traditional IRA contribution from current taxable income, you can still make a nondeductible contribution to your traditional IRA. At some income levels, part of your contribution is deductible and part is not. Any time you make a nondeductible contribution to a traditional IRA, you need to report it on Form 8606. When you begin taking distributions, the nondeductible contributions you made will escape taxation; their earnings, however, will be taxed—as will all deductible contributions and their earnings. The Roth IRA chart uses the term "contribution" rather than "deduction" because no Roth contributions are deductible.

3. Coverdell Education Savings Accounts—Parents can establish education IRAs for each child and make annual nondeductible contributions of up to $2,000 to each. This privilege is above and beyond your ability to make contributions to traditional and Roth IRAs. Earnings on education IRA funds accumulate tax-free, and tax-free withdrawals can be made to pay for elementary school, secondary school, undergraduate or graduate education expenses. This includes expenses for tuition, books, room and board, and purchase of a computer system, educational software, and Internet access.

The ability to make contributions is phased out between AGI ranges for joint filers and single taxpayers. Subject to limitations, grandparents and others can establish education IRAs to benefit grandchildren and other designated individuals.

Part 4

INVESTMENT COUNSELING

Have you ever wondered where you can go to get good investment advice? There is no "right" answer to the question. In large part, it depends on your age, income, and temperament. Options include everything from an inexpensive magazine or newsletter to very expensive professional counsel.

Before seeking investment advice, you first need to make sure you are prepared to invest. Living within your means is the first level, or foundation, of investing. You must be able to manage the money you earn in order to create a surplus to invest. This means creating a spending plan.

Everyone needs a spending plan, even those with higher incomes. It is impossible to be a good steward of what God has entrusted to you if you don't manage it well. Obviously, those with less income also need spending plans or they will never develop a surplus that can be multiplied.

Counseling for Novice Investors

Once you have a workable spending plan and develop a surplus to invest, learn as much as you can before taking any risks.

Usually, the counselors or advisors available to low-budget investors are commissioned salespeople who make their living by selling products like insurance, mutual funds, and annuities. The entry-level investor simply doesn't have enough money to buy the services of a professional investment advisor.

Therefore, novice investors have three basic options:

1. Do their own investing and pay the price of learning as they go.
2. Take the advice of salespeople and hope they sell a quality product.
3. Seek inexpensive written materials they can rely on for guidance.

Fortunately, many good materials are available to educate nonprofessional investors.

Usually, first-time investors subscribe to too many resources. This often results in confusion and frustration as one publication contradicts another. The key is to select resources that don't push a particular agenda, such as precious metals, insurance, mutual funds, etc.

Newsletters and Web sites can be a good source of basic advice. Low-budget or first-time investors should subscribe to newsletters written specifically for them. It's crucial to verify the track record of the managing editor, since usually that person is the primary advice giver. Look for a newsletter that takes the first-time investor through each phase of learning, including specific advice about what investments to use at each level of income.

In summary, potential investors should keep one important point in mind: "Let the buyer beware." Be prudent when selecting investments and always seek wise counsel. Above all, pray about every investment decision you make.

Commissioned Salespeople

The next step up in investment advice involves people who sell a product (or products) and generate commissions (as opposed to charging a fee).

This type of investment counselor varies broadly. Some are very qualified to give good, objective counsel and also earn commissions in the process. Others are novices or incompetents. They sell only what they've been taught to sell and offer little or no balance in their advice.

One way to find a good advisor is to require several references from others with whom the salesperson has worked. Check with at least three of the advisor's clients to verify his or her track record.

It is important that these clients have been dealing with the advisor for at least three years. If the advisor won't provide such references, look elsewhere for advice.

Some commissioned salespeople try to talk you into buying from them because they're Christians (or church members). And they try to make you feel guilty if you don't. Avoid them with all diligence. If an agent's products and track record will not stand by themselves, stay away. Otherwise, you'll probably lose your money as well as your friend.

Also avoid the "doom-and-gloomers," who talk about coming economic disasters and then try to sell you "collapse proof" investments, such as gold and silver.

Fee-Plus-Commission Advisors

In addition to advisors who make their incomes exclusively from commission sales, there are a growing number of investment advisors who will work either way—fees or commission sales, or both.

Usually, these advisors will initially provide counsel for a fixed fee per hour. Then, if you elect to buy products from them, they'll reduce the fee by the commissions they receive.

Prudent investors recognize that advisors usually exercise significant influence over their clients. In many instances, this means investors end up buying what the advisors recommend, which are usually the products they sell.

The question then becomes whether the fee-plus-commission is really a ploy to get clients to buy from them while thinking they are receiving objective advice. That totally depends on the character of the advisor—something you will need to discern for yourself.

A simple comparison of the value and prices of the products suggested will tell you whether the advisor is totally objective. If the investment products he or she offers are as good as those offered through other agents, then why not buy from your advisor? But if what he or she offers is inferior or higher priced, avoid the advice as well as the product.

Fee-Only Investment Advisors

A fee-only advisor is exactly what the name implies. He or she charges a fee but does not sell any products or accept commissions—usually. We say "usually" because some advisors who advertised themselves as fee-only planners accept commissions, known as "finder's fees," from product companies.

Because they generate their income from fees, you can expect fee-only advisors to be expensive. Most cater to the upper-income investor and often require a minimum level of net worth for the clients they advise. The fees can range from several hundred dollars for a one-time evaluation to several thousand a year for continuing clients.

In general, I have not found fee-only advisors to be any more accurate in their advice than a well-seasoned fee-plus-commission advisor, although there are exceptions. The one area in which fee-only planners usually excel is in designing long-term investment strategies for their clients.

Since follow-up is so essential, they usually do a good job of getting their clients to implement their plans. After all, if you're paying someone $10,000 a year to advise you, usually you'll do what they say.

Fee-Only Versus Commission

No matter which type of advisor you're considering, check out his or her track record carefully. It doesn't matter whether you pay your advisor by way of a fee or a commission. What matters is, will your advisor make more money for you than he or she will cost you?

A commissioned salesperson who makes 12 percent for clients after all commissions, administrative charges, and market fluctuations are taken into account is still better than a fee-only planner who makes 6 percent for clients after all costs.

Remember to ask for at least three local people you can talk to about your advisor's track record. If you can't get these references, look for another advisor.

Christian or Non-Christian Advisors?

Psalm 1:1-2 says, *"How blessed is the man who does not walk in the counsel of the wicked, nor stand in the path of sinners, nor sit in the seat of scoffers! But his delight is in the law of the Lord, and in His law he meditates day and night."*

There's a clear implication here that our primary source of counsel should be from those who know the Lord. Does this imply that we should never take counsel from an unbeliever? I don't think so. I believe the implication is not to rely on secular counsel as our daily source of wisdom. All counsel should be weighed against God's wisdom and discarded if it fails the test. That includes Christian and non-Christian counsel.

Where Do You Find a Good Investment Advisor?

There is no perfect formula for finding a good investment advisor, but you can make your search easier.

1. Contact *KingdomAdvisors.org* for a recommended Christian financial professional. Kingdom Advisors, led by Ron Blue and founded by Larry Burkett, is devoted to equipping Christian financial advisors to apply biblical wisdom to their advice and counsel.

2. Ask in your church and Bible studies for references. Ask people who give you references if they have made money with the advisors they are recommending. Look for an advisor with at least five years of experience (10 if possible). Anyone can guess right one time, but that doesn't establish a track record. If an advisor hasn't ridden out at least one major recession in his or her field, in my opinion that advisor is still a novice.

3. Check an advisor's credentials with the National Association of Securities Dealers if he or she is a registered broker. If this advisor has ever had his or her license suspended or revoked, be very cautious.

4. Check with several local accountants who do tax returns for people you know. Often they see the bad as well as the good side of an advisor. Although most accountants will hesitate to give a bad report on a bad advisor, most will not hesitate to give a good report on a good advisor.

5. Check to see if an advisor has earned professional designations such as CFP® (Certified Financial Planner), CLU (Chartered Life Underwriter) and ChFC (Chartered Financial Consultant). These designations won't guarantee that a particular advisor is best for you, but at the very least they show that the advisor has completed a disciplined course of study.

Discount Brokers

During the last decade or so, many discount brokerage firms have been started. These firms will place investment orders for very low commissions. This trend is certain to grow as banks expand further into the investment area.

Once you have a level of expertise that allows you the freedom to make your own investment decisions, the use of a discount broker can save you money when trading in individual stocks, bonds, mutual funds, etc.

Part 5

IMPORTANT GOALS FOR INVESTORS

Establish a "Safety Net" of Cash and Insurance

One of the most important goals to consider when you invest money is the creation of a "safety net" to provide for your family in the event of a catastrophe.

This includes a cash reserve large enough to cover three to six months of living expenses. Of course, this reserve should be in a highly liquid account. In other words, you should be able to withdraw this money easily when you need it.

Another part of your safety net should be life insurance to provide income for your family in the event of your death. Having insurance and a cash reserve reduces the likelihood of needing to sell a long-term investment prematurely or at an inopportune time.

Get Started Early

When you start investing early in life, you spread the task of accumulating funds over a longer period of time. For example, suppose you want to accumulate $300,000 by age 65. Assuming a 10 percent compounded rate of return, you'll need to put away $47 per month if you begin investing at age 25.

If you begin at 35, you'll need to put away $133 per month. At age 45, the monthly amount is $395. And at 55, it jumps to $1,464.

Investing early in life depends on how much surplus a young couple or single person has. The amount of surplus depends on lifestyle.

Unfortunately, too many young people jump head over heels into debt by purchasing homes that are far too expensive for their income. Then, they add to their debt load by purchasing high-priced adult toys like luxury cars, boats, and swimming pools. As a consequence, they can't pay off their mortgage early, and they have little or no money to set aside in a company retirement account.

In Part 1 we noted that early repayment of your house mortgage should be your first investment priority. We made an exception for a company retirement account with matching funds of at least 25 percent.

Living beyond your means will make it impossible to pay off your mortgage early or make any other meaningful investment. Accepting a less expensive house can make all the difference, allowing you to pay it off early and then have plenty of money available to invest.

How quickly can you retire a mortgage? Let's use the example of a $100,000 mortgage at 10 percent for 30 years. By paying only $100 extra per month toward the principal you can retire that mortgage about 11 years early and save $113,000 in interest!

Give Your Money the Freedom to Grow

The more constraints you place on your investment program, the more likely it is that your investment results will fail to meet your expectations. Earning too little on your investments is one of the greatest obstacles to investment success, along with starting too late. It is important that you keep pace with inflation.

It's not enough just to preserve what you have now. You need to make your money grow just to stay even with the rising cost of living. Let's consider the effect of inflation over the last 82 years. The average rate of inflation over 82 years (1926 to 2007) has been 3.0 percent annually. What you could buy for $1 in 1926 now costs $12.00 according to the Ibbotson.®

Let's apply this to retirement savings. If you assume (could be dangerous) that future inflation will mirror the past, you know that your monthly income will need to grow every year in order to keep the same purchasing power. If you think you can retire comfortably on $4,000 per month beginning now, in 30 years your $4,000 per month would need to be $9,827 per month. Sobering, isn't it?

This is not to suggest that you pour all your money into a high-risk investment with a high rate of return. But on the other hand, you wouldn't want to invest all your money in T-bills. The "Rule of 72" is a useful tool in demonstrating the importance of your investment return. Simply divide 72 by the rate of return, and the quotient will tell you how many years it will take for your investment value to double.

Let's assume your rate of return is 6 percent. If you divide 72 by 6, the quotient is 12. So, it will take 12 years for your investment value to double with a 6 percent rate of return. Now, let's assume your rate of return is 12 percent. If you divide 72 by 12, the quotient is 6. By doubling your rate of return, you cut in half the years required to double your investment.

It should be obvious at this point that, over the long haul, bank savings accounts and CDs are not the best place for all of your investment dollars. And the portion of your money that you do invest at the bank doesn't necessarily have to go into a CD or savings account. Investigate money market accounts, and compare various bank rates because they can vary considerably from product to product and institution to institution.

Use Strategies That Provide Safety and Return

Using some higher-risk investments to help counter the effects of inflation does not mean throwing caution to the wind. The risks associated with these investments can be reduced enough to satisfy most investors. The solution is to use risk-minimizing strategies. Several are listed below.

Diversification

Discussed in Part 1 (Key #6).

Professional Management

One way to avoid investment errors is to have your investment portfolio managed by a qualified professional, which can be a costly proposition. But even if you have just a small amount of money to invest, there's still a way to get the benefits of professional management. That's what mutual funds provide.

Since mutual funds vary tremendously in performance—even within their own category—shop carefully to select funds that consistently perform at or near the top of their category. Financial magazines regularly list these. Online brokerages typically have powerful screening tools that will help you find the best funds.

Investing for the Long Term

Discussed in Part 1 (Key #7).

Asset Allocation

This means dividing your investment dollars into percentages, which you then put into different groups of investments. You might want to use the five tiers described in Part 2.

For example, you might put 20 percent of your money into Tier I, which is Secure Income. You might put 40 percent into Tier II (Long-Term Income), 30 percent into Tier III (Growth Investments), 10 percent into Tier IV (Speculative Growth Investments), and nothing into Tier V (High Risk Investments).

The younger you are, the more likely you will want to have higher percentages in Tier III and IV investments, but the percentage you put into each tier will depend on your individual goals, needs, philosophy, and risk tolerance.

Dollar Cost Averaging

Consistency is important if you want the best return on your investment dollar. Dollar cost averaging means that you regularly add a certain amount into a particular investment.

For example, you might want to set aside $50 per month to invest in a mutual fund or buy shares of stock in a particular company. Each investment you made in the mutual fund would buy a certain number of shares in the fund, depending on what the share price was at that particular time. Both the share prices for stocks and mutual funds would fluctuate.

The following example shows the benefits of dollar cost averaging in a market in which share prices are declining. In this example, the regular investment is $200, which is made once per quarter.

Quarter Amount	Quarterly Price	Share Purchased	Shares
1st Qtr.	$200	$25.00	8
2nd Qtr.	$200	$20.00	10
3rd Qtr.	$200	$12.50	16
4th Qtr.	$200	$10.00	20
Total:	$800	$67.50	54

Average quarterly price per share ($67.50 ÷ 4) = $16.88
Price per share with dollar cost averaging ($800 ÷ 54) = $14.81

Puzzling? This lower cost per share with dollar cost averaging occurs because you get more shares for your $200 when the price is lower.

Perhaps the bigger question is: Would you want to keep buying this stock? Maybe. Some pros would say yes and others would say no, depending on the situation, but that's one of the reasons a mutual fund provides more comfort. It's less volatile, and dollar cost averaging works just the same.

Build from Quality

Investing is like building a reserve for the future. Be sure the products you select are quality products.

10 WRAPPING IT UP WITH HOPE

Insurance and investing can be intimidating subjects because of their complexity, but both are intended to be your friends. They exist to improve the quality of your life and to help you manage the resources God has entrusted to your care.

Rather than let a lack of knowledge paralyze you or fill you with fear, recognize it as a temporary condition that can be cured. God encourages us to look to Him for wisdom and to ask with confidence: *"But if any of you lacks wisdom, let him ask of God, who gives to all generously and without reproach, and it will be given to him"* (James 1:5).

God's direction is not likely to come in a heavenly billboard listing policy specifications and stocks to buy, but don't underestimate its value.

- He has gifted others within His body with detailed insurance and investment knowledge.

- He has directed you to seek their counsel.

- He has given you a mind with which to make decisions.

- His Spirit illuminates your mind regarding His purposes for you.

- He wants you to trust Him (attitude) and be a good steward (action).

It is comforting to know that Jesus, through direct experience, can identify with our weaknesses. *"For we do not have a high priest who cannot sympathize with our weaknesses, but One who has been tempted in all things as we are, yet without sin"* (Hebrews 4:15).

It's even more comforting to know that after overcoming weaknesses and temptations, He didn't wash His hands of us and declare us unfit for companionship. Instead, He valued us enough to give His life in exchange for ours and then to give us His never-ending presence in the form of His Spirit to reside inside of us.

How should we respond? *"Therefore let us draw near with confidence to the throne of grace, so that we may receive mercy and find grace to help in time of need"* (Hebrews 4:16).

How great is that! God is waiting to meet your requests with mercy and grace, illuminating your path as you grow in trust and obedience.

Action Steps

_____

_____

_____

_____

_____

_____

Celebration Plan

_____

_____

_____

_____

_____

_____

APPENDIX

INTRODUCTION TO CHRIST

As important as our financial welfare is, it is not our highest priority. The single most important need of every person everywhere is to know God and experience the gift of His forgiveness and peace.

These five biblical truths will show you God's open door through a personal relationship with Jesus Christ.

1. God loves you and wants you to know Him and experience a meaningful life.

God created people in His own image, and He desires a close relationship with each of us. *"For God so loved the world, that He gave His only begotten Son, that whoever believes in Him shall not perish, but have eternal life"* (John 3:16). *"I [Jesus] came that they might have life, and have it abundantly"* (John 10:10).

God the Father loved you so much that He gave His only Son, Jesus Christ, to die for you.

2. Unfortunately, we are separated from God.

Because God is holy and perfect, no sin can abide in His presence. Every person has sinned, and the consequence of sin is separation from God. *"All have sinned and fall short of the glory of God"* (Romans 3:23). *"Your sins have cut you off from God"* (Isaiah 59:2, TLB).

3. God's only provision to bridge this gap is Jesus Christ.

Jesus Christ died on the cross to pay the penalty for our sin, bridging the gap between God and us. Jesus said, *"I am the way, and the truth, and the life; no one comes to the Father but through Me"* (John 14:6). *"God demonstrates His own love towards us, in that while we were yet sinners, Christ died for us"* (Romans 5:8).

4. This relationship is a gift from God.

Our efforts can never achieve the perfection God requires. The only solution was to provide it to us as a gift.

When Jesus bore our sins on the cross, paying our penalty forever, He exchanged His righteousness for our guilt. By faith, we receive the gift we could never deserve.

Is that fair? Of course not! God's love exceeds His justice, resulting in mercy and grace toward us.

"It is by grace you have been saved, through faith—and this is not from yourselves, it is the gift of God—not by works, so that no one can boast" (Ephesians 2:8-9, NIV).

5. We must each receive Jesus Christ individually.

Someone has said that God has no grandchildren. Each of us is responsible before God for our own sin. We can continue to bear the responsibility and pay the consequences or we can receive the gift of Jesus' righteousness, enabling God to declare us "Not guilty!"

If you desire to know the Lord and are not certain whether you have this relationship, we encourage you to receive Christ right now. Pray a prayer similar to this suggested one:

"God, I need You. I invite Jesus to come into my life as my Savior and Lord and to make me the person You want me to be. Thank You for forgiving my sins and for giving me the gift of eternal life."

You may be successful in avoiding financial quicksand—and we pray you will be—but without a relationship with Christ, it won't have lasting value. Eternal perspective begins with Him.

If you ask Christ into your life, please tell some people you know who are also following Christ. They will encourage you and help you get involved in a Bible-teaching church where you can grow spiritually. And please let us know as well. We would love to help in any way we can.

2 GOD'S OWNERSHIP & FINANCIAL FAITHFULNESS

How we view God determines how we live. Viewing Him as Savior is a good beginning, but growth comes when we view Him as Lord.

After losing his children and all his possessions, Job continued to worship God because he knew God was the Lord of those possessions and retained the ultimate rights over them. Realizing that God owed him nothing and he owed God everything enabled him to submit to God's authority and find contentment.

Moses walked away from his earthly inheritance, regarding *"disgrace for the sake of Christ as of greater value than the treasures of Egypt"* because he had his eye on God's reward (Hebrews 11:26, NIV).

Our willingness, like theirs, to give up a lesser value for a greater one, requires recognizing what most of the world does not: God is not only the Creator and Owner of all but also the ultimate definer of value. Those responsibilities belong to Him. He has retained them because He alone is capable of handling them.

Most of the frustration we experience in handling money comes when we take God's responsibilities on our own shoulders. Successful money management requires us to understand three aspects of God's Lordship—three roles for which He retains responsibility.

1. GOD OWNS IT ALL.

God owns all our possessions. *"To the Lord your God belong . . . the earth and everything in it"* (Deuteronomy 10:14, NIV). *"The earth is the Lord's, and all it contains"* (Psalm 24:1).

Leviticus 25:23 identifies Him as the owner of all the land: *"The land . . . shall not be sold permanently, for the land is Mine."* Haggai 2:8 says that He owns the precious metals: *"'The silver is Mine and the gold is Mine,' declares the Lord of hosts."*

Even our body—the one thing for which we would tend to claim total ownership—is not our own. *"Or do you not know that your body is a temple of the Holy Spirit who is in you, whom you have from God, and that you are not your own?"* (1 Corinthians 6:19).

The Lord created all things, and He never transferred the ownership of His creation to people. In Colossians 1:17 we are told that, *"In Him all things hold together."* At this very moment the Lord holds everything together by His power. As we will see throughout this study, recognizing God's ownership is crucial in allowing Jesus Christ to become the Lord of our money and possessions.

• Yielding Our Ownership to His Lordship

If we are to be genuine followers of Christ, we must transfer ownership of our possessions to Him. *"None of you can be My disciple who does not give up all his own possessions"* (Luke 14:33). Sometimes He tests us by asking us to give up the very possessions that are most important to us.

The most vivid example of this in Scripture is when God instructed Abraham, *"Take now your son, your only son, whom you love, Isaac . . . and offer him there as a burnt offering"* (Genesis 22:2). When Abraham obeyed, demonstrating his willingness to give up his most valuable possession, God responded, *"Do not lay a hand on the boy . . . now I know that you fear God, because you have not withheld from Me your son"* (Genesis 22:12, NIV).

When we acknowledge God's ownership, every spending decision becomes a spiritual decision. No longer do we ask, "Lord, what do You want me to do with my money?" It becomes, "Lord, what do You want me to do with Your money?" When we have this attitude and handle His money according to His wishes, spending and saving decisions become as spiritual as giving decisions.

• Recognizing God's Ownership

Our culture—the media, even the law—says that what you possess, you own. Acknowledging God's ownership requires a transformation of thinking, and this can be difficult. Many people say that God owns it all while they cling desperately to possessions that they think define them.

Here are a number of practical suggestions to help us recognize God's ownership.

- For the next 30 days, meditate on 1 Chronicles 29:11-12 when you first awake and just before going to sleep.

- For the next 30 days, ask God to make you aware of His ownership and help you to be thankful for it.

- Establish the habit of acknowledging God's ownership every time you buy something.

Recognizing God's ownership is important in learning contentment. When you believe you own something, you are more vulnerable to its circumstances. If it suffers loss or damage, your attitude can swing quickly from happy to discontented.

Recognizing it as God's loss doesn't make it irrelevant, but it does change your perspective. Now you can focus on how He will use this incident in causing *"all things to work together for good to those who love God, to those who are called according to His purpose"* (Romans 8:28).

2. GOD CONTROLS IT ALL.

Besides being Creator and Owner, God is ultimately in control of every event that occurs upon the earth. *"We adore you as being in control of everything"* (1 Chronicles 29:11, TLB). *"Whatever the Lord pleases, He does, in heaven and in earth"* (Psalm 135:6). And in the book of Daniel, King Nebuchadnezzar stated: *"I praised the Most High; I honored and glorified him who lives forever. . . . He does as he pleases with the powers of heaven and the peoples of the earth. No one can hold back his hand or say to him: 'What have you done?'"* (Daniel 4:34-35, NIV).

God is also in control of difficult events. *"I am the Lord, and there is no other, the One forming light and creating darkness, causing well-being and creating calamity; I am the Lord who does all these"* (Isaiah 45:6-7).

It is important for us to realize that our heavenly Father uses even seemingly devastating circumstances for ultimate good in the lives of the godly. *"We know that God causes all things to work together for good to those who love God, to those who are called according to His purpose"* (Romans 8:28). God allows difficult circumstances for three reasons.

- **He accomplishes His intentions.**

This is illustrated in the life of Joseph, who was sold into slavery as a teenager by his jealous brothers. Joseph later said to his brothers: *"Do not be distressed and do not be angry with yourselves for selling me here, because it was to save lives that God sent me ahead of you. . . . It was not you who sent me here, but God. . . . You intended to harm me, but God intended it for good to accomplish what is now being done, the saving of many lives"* (Genesis 45:5, 8; 50:20, NIV).

- **He develops our character.**

Godly character, something that is precious in His sight, is often developed during trying times. *"We also rejoice in our sufferings, because we know that suffering produces perseverance; perseverance, character"* (Romans 5:3-4, NIV).

- **He disciplines His children.**

"Those whom the Lord loves He disciplines. . . . He disciplines us for our good, so that we may share His holiness. All discipline for the moment seems not to be joyful, but sorrowful; yet to those who have been trained by it, afterwards it yields the peaceful fruit of righteousness" (Hebrews 12:6,10-11).

When we are disobedient, we can expect our loving Lord to discipline us, often through difficult circumstances. His purpose is to encourage us to abandon our sin and to "share His holiness."

You can be at peace knowing that your loving heavenly Father is in control of every situation you will ever face. He will use every one of them for a good purpose.

3. GOD PROVIDES IT ALL.

God promises to provide our needs. *"Seek first His kingdom and His righteousness, and all these things [food and clothing] will be added to you"* (Matthew 6:33).

The same God who fed manna to the children of Israel during their 40 years of wandering in the wilderness and who fed 5,000 with only five loaves and two fish has promised to provide our needs. This is the same God who told Elijah, *"I have commanded the ravens to provide for you there. . . . The ravens brought him bread and meat in the morning and bread and meat in the evening"*
(1 Kings 17:4, 6).

God—Both Predictable and Unpredictable

God is totally predictable in His faithfulness to provide for our needs. What we cannot predict is how He will provide. He uses various and often surprising means—an increase in income or a gift. He may provide an opportunity to stretch limited resources through money-saving purchases. Regardless of how He chooses to provide for our needs, He is completely reliable.

Our culture believes that God plays no part in financial matters; they assume that His invisibility means He is uninvolved. They try to shoulder responsibilities that God never intended for them—burdens of ownership, control, and provision that only He can carry.

Jesus said, *"Come to Me, all who are weary and heavy-laden, and I will give you rest. Take My yoke upon you. . . . For My yoke is easy, and My burden is light"* (Matthew 11:28-30). This is the only way we can rest and enjoy the peace of God.

When we trust God to do His part in our finances, we can focus on doing our part: being financially faithful with every resource He has given us.

Defining Financial Faithfulness

Faithfully living by God's financial principles doesn't necessarily mean having a pile of money in the bank, but it does bring an end to overdue bills and their related stress. And that's not the most important part; that's just relief from symptoms.

Consider some of the big-picture benefits:

- Assurance that God is in control of our circumstances
- Absolute faith in His promise to meet all of our needs
- A clear conscience before God
- A clear conscience with others

This is not to say that we will live on financial autopilot with no more challenges for the rest of our lives. God promises no such thing. In fact, without challenges our faith has no opportunity to be perfected or even to grow; without challenges it isn't active or visible. But peace in the midst of challenges is a miraculous quality of life, and that's what God promises when we learn to trust and follow Him fully.

With God in control, we have nothing to fear. He is the Master of the universe. His wisdom is superior to ours in every way, and no situation is too complex or hopeless for Him to solve.

God has even provided a solution for our ongoing frailties and failings. As part of His great redemption, He offers continuing forgiveness and cleansing from all unrighteousness (1 John 1:9). We make mistakes—sometimes willfully violating His plan for us—but He welcomes our confession and honors it by restoring our fellowship and renewing our guidance.

Once we begin to experience the rewards of financial faithfulness, we never want to be without them. Our deepening trust in *God's* faithfulness intensifies our desire to stay within His will, resulting in perfect peace.

Many people have inherited or achieved financial independence: a level of wealth that requires no further work or income. But apart from Christ, they don't have freedom from anxiety; they have merely replaced one set of worries with another. They often fear:

- Loss of what they have accumulated
- Loss of meaningful relationships — fearing that others only care about what they have rather than who they are
- Loss of safety as their wealth makes them a target for theft or kidnapping
- Loss of grace from others, who jealously hold them to a higher standard because of their wealth

Being financially free, on the other hand, includes freedom from these fears as well as from the oppression of envy, covetousness, and greed.

Financial faithfulness is transformation — a process that requires God's power and our participation. It is synonymous with our definition of true financial faithfulness in the *Crown Money Map™*:

1. Knowing that God owns it all.
2. Finding contentment with what He provides.
3. Being free to be all He made you to be.

This is the big picture, the framework within which wealth and material possessions take their rightful place — not as ends but as means — in God's hands.

Steps to Cultivate Financial Faithfulness

Now it is time to outline the path. Since we're talking about transformation, you'll notice that some of our steps go well beyond mere money-management techniques.

1. TRANSFER OWNERSHIP.

Transferring ownership of every possession to God means acknowledging that He already owns them and that we will begin treating them accordingly. This includes more than just material possessions; it includes money, time, family, education, even earning potential for the future. This is essential to experience the Spirit-filled life in the area of finances (see Psalm 8:4-6).

There is no substitute for this step. If we believe we are the owners of even a single possession, then the events affecting that possession are going to affect our attitudes. God will not input His perfect will into our lives unless we first surrender our wills to Him.

However, if we make a total transfer of everything to God, He will demonstrate His ability. It is important to understand and accept God's conditions for His control (see Deuteronomy 5:32-33). God will keep His promise to provide our every need according to His perfect plan.

It is easy to say we will make a total transfer of everything to God, but it's not so easy to do. Our desire for control and our habit of self-management cause difficulty in consistently seeking God's will in the area of material things. But without a deep conviction that He is in control, we can never experience true financial faithfulness.

What a great relief it is to turn our burdens over to Him. Then, if something happens to the car, we can say, "Father, I gave this car to You; I've maintained it to the best of my ability, but I don't own it. It belongs to You, so do with it whatever You like." Then look for the blessing God has in store as a result of this attitude.

2. BECOME DEBT FREE.

God wants us to be free to serve Him without restriction. *"You were bought with a price; do not become slaves of men"* (1 Corinthians 7:23). *"The rich rules over the poor, and the borrower becomes the lender's slave"* (Proverbs 22:7).

For most, this will involve sacrifice—at least initially—but the payoff is well worth it.

3. GIVE REGULARLY AND GENEROUSLY.

Every follower of Christ should establish tithing (10 percent of income) as a beginning point of giving and as a testimony to God's ownership. We can't say we have given total ownership to God if our actions don't back the claim.

It is through sharing that we bring His power in finances into focus. In every case, God wants us to give the first part to Him, but He also wants us to pay our creditors. This requires establishing a plan, and it will probably mean making sacrifices of wants and desires until all obligations are current.

We cannot sacrifice God's part—that is not our prerogative as faithful, obedient followers of Christ. Malachi 3:8-9 has strong words for those who "rob God." But then verses 10-12 describe His great blessing for those who tithe fully.

God, as the first giver, wants us to be like Him, and His economy rewards our generosity. *"Now this I say, he who sows sparingly will also reap sparingly, and he who sows bountifully will also reap bountifully"* (2 Corinthians 9:6).

Steps two and three combine to form an important conclusion. If, while en route to financial faithfulness, sacrifice becomes necessary—and it almost always does—our sacrifice must not come from God's or our creditor's share. We must choose areas within our other discretionary expenses to sacrifice. Consider it an opportunity to exercise faith in God's reward for our obedience.

4. ACCEPT GOD'S PROVISION.

To obtain financial peace, recognize and accept that God's provision is used to direct each of our lives. Often Christians lose sight of the fact that God's will can be accomplished through a withholding of funds; we think that He can direct us only by an abundance of money. But God does not choose for everyone to live in great abundance. This does not imply poverty, but it may mean that God wants us to be more responsive to His day-by-day control.

Followers of Christ must learn to live on what God provides and not give in to a driving desire for wealth or the pressure brought on by comparison with others. This necessitates planning our lifestyle within the provision God has supplied. When we are content to do this, God will always help us find a way.

5. KEEP A CLEAR CONSCIENCE.

Living with integrity means dealing with the past as well as the present. Part of becoming financially faithful requires gaining a clear conscience regarding past business practices and personal dealings. Sometimes, in addition to a changed attitude, our transformation means making restitution for situations where we have wronged someone.

Tim's story is a good example. Before he accepted Christ, he cheated someone out of some money. God convicted him about this and indicated that he should go and make restitution. He contacted the person, confessed what had been done, and offered to make it right. The person refused to forgive and also refused to take any money.

Tim's ego and pride were hurt until he realized that he had been both obedient and successful. His confession was not primarily for the offended person but for his own relationship with God. He had done exactly what God had asked, and God had forgiven him. Nothing further was required.

6. PUT OTHERS FIRST.

This does not imply being a door mat; it simply means that we shouldn't profit at the unfair expense of someone else. As is often the case, attitude is all-important.

7. MANAGE TIME PRIORITIES.

A workaholic might gain wealth at the expense of the family's relational needs, but wealth alone is no indicator of financial faithfulness. And wealth gained with wrong priorities is likely to vanish. *"Do not weary yourself to gain wealth, cease from your consideration of it. When you set your eyes on it, it is gone. For wealth certainly makes itself wings like an eagle that flies toward the heavens"* (Proverbs 23:4-5). Even if it doesn't vanish, it can't deliver the satisfaction it promises. Don't be deceived by overcommitment to business or the pursuit of wealth.

God's priorities for us are very clear.

Priority number one is to develop our relationship with Jesus Christ.

Priority number two is our family. This includes teaching them God's Word. And that requires quality time, something that can't exist without a sufficient quantity from which to flow.

Develop the habit of a regular time to study God's Word for yourself as well as a family time that acknowledges your commitment to each other and to God.

Turn off the television, have the children do their homework early, and begin to study the Bible together. Pray for each other and for those in need. Help your children become intercessors who can pray for others and expect God to answer.

Priority number three is your work, which God intends to be an opportunity for ministry and personal development in addition to providing an income.

Priority number four is church activities and other ministry. This does not imply that it is unimportant or can be neglected, but it keeps us from using church as an excuse to let higher priorities slide.

If we observe priority number one, we will not neglect our church.

8. AVOID OVER-INDULGENCE.

Jesus said, *"If anyone wishes to come after Me, he must deny himself, and take up his cross daily and follow Me"* (Luke 9:23). Once again, this is about priorities. Who wins the contest between God's claim on your life and your own pursuit of pleasure?

In Philippians 3:18-19, Paul says that many live as the enemies of the cross of Christ, and he describes them by saying, *"Their destiny is destruction, their god is their stomach, and their glory is in their shame"* (NIV).

That sounds alarmingly like much of our culture, and it takes great effort to avoid being swept along with the current.

9. GET CHRISTIAN COUNSEL.

"Without consultation, plans are frustrated, but with many counselors they succeed" (Proverbs 15:22). God admonishes us to seek counsel and not to rely solely on our own resources. People are often frustrated in financial planning because they lack the necessary knowledge. A common but tragic response is to give up. Within the body of Christ, God has supplied those who have the ability to help in the area of finances. Seek Christian counselors.

To read more on what God says about handling money, go to Crown.org.

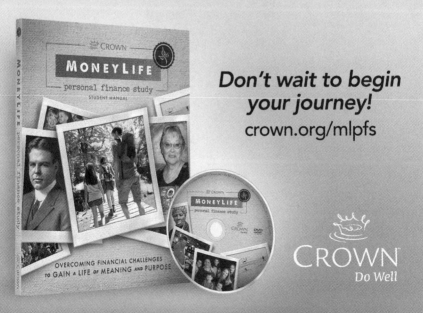

About Crown

Crown's mission is to equip servant leaders to live by God's design for their finances, work and life...to advance transformation. We strive to see the followers of Christ in every nation faithfully living by God's financial principles in every area of their life so they are free to serve Him more fully. As an interdenominational Christian ministry, Crown serves people seeking to improve their personal finances, businesses and careers.

Crown employs a variety of media, including dramatic films, video, radio, podcasts, seminars and small group studies to achieve this end. Our mission is accomplished through a global network of dedicated staff and volunteers.

Founded in 1976, Crown Financial Ministries is a 501(c)(3) nonprofit educational organization. Headquartered in Knoxville, Tennessee, Crown has operations in cities across the United States and is active on five continents.

We invite you to get acquainted with us. It is our privilege to serve you.

CROWN
Do Well

crown.org